Alien Intervention

ALIEN INTERVENTION

The Spiritual Mission of UFOs

by

Paul Christopher

Huntington House Publishers

Huntington House Publishers
P.O. Box 53788
Lafayette, Louisiana 70505

Library of Congress Card Catalog Number
97-77563
ISBN 1-56384-148-7

Dedication

This book is dedicated to
my wonderful son
Trenton.

Contents

Acknowledgments

Many dedicated researchers have labored to tackle this enigmatic subject. Without their diligent efforts that have gone on before me, this book would not have been written. Heartfelt thanks go to Jerome Clark, Scott Corrales, Tony Dodd, Raymond E. Fowler, Salvador Freixedo, Allen H. Greenfield, Linda Moulton Howe, David M. Jacobs, John A. Keel, Jim Keith, Jorge Martin, Dr. Malachi Martin, J. Gordon Melton, Margaret Sachs, and Jacques Vallee.

In addition, I would especially like to thank Pastor Tom Vasiliow for his editing expertise and his theological advice and insights.

All praise and glory go to my Lord and Saviour, Jesus Christ. The power of His Holy Spirit has enlightened me during this eye-opening journey into the unknown.

Introduction

Something unimaginable is going on! It involves our entire planet, yet hardly anyone realizes it. Most of us are busy trying to make a living, raise a family, or get an education, and therefore do not recognize its mechanism. We only see what is on the surface because that is all we are supposed to see. We assume that we're getting all the facts, when, in actuality, what we are seeing and hearing is merely the tip of the iceberg—just a glimpse of what is really going on.

We are, however, being conditioned to think a certain way and to accept certain beliefs. It is an ongoing process that began a long time ago. It is targeting everyone, especially the children. It is affecting millions globally.

UFOs, UFO contacts, alien abductions, animal mutilations, crop circles, some visions of the Blessed Virgin Mary, psychic phenomena, the supernatural, religion, the occult, numerology, astrology, science, politics, the United States government and military, television, and certain key individuals (along with the general public) are collectively instrumental in fueling its *sinister* plan.

This book seeks to uncover and reveal the startling truth regarding why UFO events are occurring worldwide. It examines and details who is being contacted and for what reason, how specific organizations are formed to aid and promulgate an "alien" scheme, and what the complex underlying purpose is of this cosmic intrusion that has plagued humanity for some fifty years. The startling evidence presented points to these activities culminating into some fantastic near-future event.

The hidden agenda cannot remain hidden. The "secret mission" must no longer remain a secret. Questions that have arisen over decades must be finally addressed. The truth is out there. It must be told.

Chapter 1

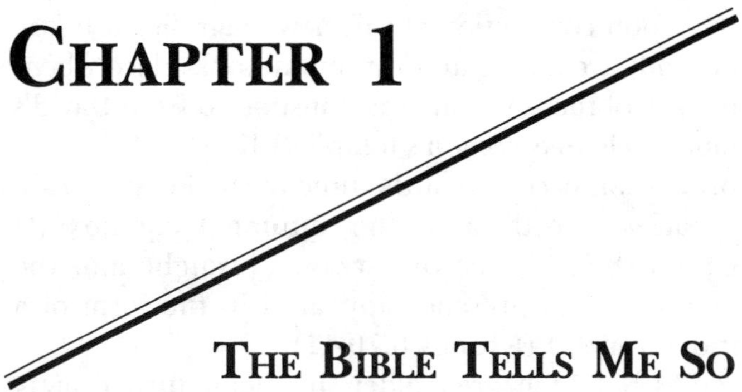

The Bible Tells Me So

Since the early 1950s, an entity named Ashtar, who claims to be from outer space, has been deliberately contacting certain individuals by means of channeling, telepathy, trance mediums, and ouija boards, offering salvation, and an assortment of other amazing things, to humankind. Ashtar, who supposedly is orbiting the earth in a huge spaceship, ranks himself "Commander in Chief of the Free Federation of Planets." This entity has recently written a book (*channeled* through a New York businessman) titled *The New World Order* that focuses on astounding predictions regarding the future of humanity.

From the years 962-922 B.C., Solomon majestically reigned as Israel's third king. Born of royal blood, he was the second son of David and Bathsheba. His regal life meticulously unfolds in the Old Testament of the Bible.

While Solomon worshiped the Lord at an ancient high place known as Gibeon, which lies eight miles northwest of Jerusalem, God appeared and spoke with Solomon in a vivid dream (I Kings 3:4-5). Solomon later devoted seven years of his life to undertake the erecting of the sacred Temple (I Kings 5:5; 6:38).

Upon completion of this new magnificent house of God, a congregated ceremony took place where the ark of the covenant was transported from David's tabernacle to Solomon's temple (I Kings 8:1-9). This procession occurred at the time of the Feast of Tabernacles, shortly after the autumnal equinox (II Chron. 8:13). After the ark was brought into the temple, God's presence appeared in the form of a radiant cloud (I Kings 8:10-11).

As Solomon grew older, his heart turned away from God, and he began worshipping false gods (I Kings 11:4-6, 33). Prior to this, one of the false deities, named Ashtaroth (or Ashtoreth), had been exerting influence over the children of Israel as well as another Old Testament leader named Samuel, who lived over two hundred years before Solomon. Samuel anointed Saul, who became the first king of Israel, and he then anointed David, who ruled as Israel's second king.

The children of Israel were constantly disobeying God's laws and flirting with false gods, including Ashtaroth who were continually surrounding them (Joshua 24:23; Judges 2:11-13; 10:6). Samuel strongly urged the children of Israel to rid themselves of Ashtaroth and the other strange gods (I Sam. 7:3-4). Samuel's devoted faith in God endured, but Solomon's heart swayed toward the evil influences that encompassed him. Solomon constructed a high worship place near Jerusalem for Ashtaroth and for two other strange gods (II Kings 23:13).

Coincidence?

Is the similarity in the spelling of the names of these two entities, Ashtar and Ashtaroth, just a coincidence? It is more likely that we have, in fact, identified the same character. John A. Keel, a prominent

UFO researcher, also uncovered this revealing similarity (Keel 1970).

Interestingly enough, we now have an entity originating from Old Testament times who is linked to today's UFO phenomenon. There are actually numerous cases where the UFO phenomenon appears to be tied to something, or someone, from the Bible. As we follow the phenomenon from the 1940s to the present, we will see how frequently religious connections emerge.

The Solomon Islands are located just east of Papua, New Guinea, in the southwest Pacific Ocean. In August 1942, during the battles of World War II, United States Marine Sergeant Stephen J. Brickner and a group of soldiers landed on Guadalcanal in the Solomon Islands. They spotted in the sky a rectangular formation of 150 unidentified silvery objects with no wings or tails.

On 29 August 1942 in Columbus, Mississippi, control tower operator Michael Solomon witnessed two round, reddish objects descending near the Army (Air Corps) Flying School. The UFOs hovered, accelerated, and then sped away.

Is it just another coincidence that the legendary biblical name *Solomon* appears on the same month (August) of the same year (1942), in two separate UFO reports? John Keel also testifies to similar coincidences surrounding the UFO phenomenon (Keel 1975a).

Throughout this book, four specific coincidences will become clearly visible:

1. Persons involved with UFO related events can have the same or a similar first, last, or middle name of another person involved with a UFO event (Keel 1975a).

2. Persons involved with UFO related events can have a name that is in the Bible, that closely resembles a biblical name, or that relates to a common biblical term.

3. Curiously, UFO sightings, abductions, and contacts often occur on the same days of the month or on the same exact date a year or years later (Keel 1975).

4. UFO incidents also occur near or at the same geographical locations year after year (Keel 1971).

The Bible informs us that around one thousand years before Christ was born, Ashtaroth and other strange powerful gods were interacting with humanity, resulting in humankind forsaking God and following after false gods. Today, Ashtar and a host of other ennobled entities who claim they are of extraterrestrial origin are spoon-feeding us some absurd intergalactic gospel of salvation. Are the strange gods of the Old Testament deceiving us into thinking that they are aliens from some other planet?

Suppose a silvery disc one hundred feet in diameter were to land in a field near your backyard. And, suppose a glorious being were to step out and tell you they are from another galaxy; would you believe this? (Then again, you might be zapped, and you wouldn't have a choice!)

If a huge spacecraft were to land in Rome, followed by similar landings in Washington, D.C., Tokyo, Beijing, and Moscow, do you think that the television media would cover it? After all, the majority of people believe what they see and hear on television.

Now suppose an "all-knowing," intergalactic traveler who purports to possess universal wisdom from afar steps out of this huge spaceship that has landed in Rome. He not only speaks with his tongue, but simultaneously communicates telepathically to all of humanity. He proposes some sort of alliance between him and his space people and the major nations of the earth. He offers us world peace, an end to starvation, and the cure for all diseases, including AIDS. But in exchange for what? Our souls? He helps us set up a one-world government, a one-world religion, and promises a life of peace and harmony. Has the human mind not created a similar storyline? Are we not anticipating this type of cosmic intervention as we plunge headlong into the twenty-first century?

It is an established fact that today millions of Christians believe in the Second Coming of Jesus Christ and that this long-awaited intervention is very close at hand. Will the aliens cunningly stage what appears to be the second coming of Christ?

The Location Factor

In 1952, between 11:40 P.M. on 19 July and 5:00 A.M. on 20 July, Washington, D.C. was the location of one of the most dramatic events in UFO history. Eight UFOs were reported visually and on radar performing erratic maneuvers in the night skies above the White House and the Capitol. Immediately, jet fighters were dispatched, but when they reached the scene, the UFOs disappeared. Uncannily, when the jet fighters left, the UFOs reappeared.

Exactly one week later, from 9:00 P.M. on 26 July until 6:00 A.M. on 27 July, between six and twelve UFOs repeated similar movements over Washington, D.C. Are we being lead to believe that a technologically-advanced extraterrestrial civilization is superior to us? Just how did our national defense officials react to these events?

In December of 1964, nearly twelve years later, UFOs reappeared around Washington, D.C. for two consecutive months. Once again, they were reported visually and on radar. Then on 21 December, a Virginia man witnessed the landing of a huge cone-shaped craft near U.S. Highway 250 between Staunton and Waynesboro. On 11 January 1965 UFOs gave an encore performance in the skies en-route to the Capitol. Two jet fighters were summoned, but the UFOs sped away.

There was a remarkable episode that was widely publicized in European newspapers in 1954. On 17 September in Rome, around 6:30 P.M., thousands of astonished people, including military officers and pilots, watched a UFO perform incredible maneuvers over the city for more than an hour. This unusual object, which left a luminous trail, was also tracked on radar.

Again, in Rome on October 28 (the following month), dozens of witnesses, including Clare Boothe Luce, a United States Congresswoman serving as ambassador to Italy, observed a luminous sphere speeding across the sky. The UFO emitted a trail of angels' hair. (Angels' hair is a white, fiber-like substance, similar to cobwebs, which sometimes falls from the sky in large quantities accompanying UFO sightings. It is composed of boron, calcium, magnesium, and silicon and disintegrates rapidly.)

In 1958 and 1959 in and around Papua, New Guinea, there were more than sixty sightings of UFOs. On 26 , 27 and 28 June 1959, at the Boianai mission in Papua, a constant display of spaceships was seen by thirty-eight people (seven were adults). The first two days, witnesses observed four occupants on top of one of the crafts apparently working on something. On the second day, to everyone's amazement, the occupants mimicked specific gestures that were directed at them by the spectators (i.e., waving, raising both arms). Father William Booth Gill, an Anglican priest who was in charge of the mission, and his assistant Stephen Gill Moi, a native teacher there, were the primary witnesses. Why was this youthful Christian congregation the target of this celestial event?

The Arrival

On 28 March 1950, a group of naked "Venusians," including ten men, ten women, and twenty-five children, staged an event for Samuel Eaton Thompson of Centralia, Washington, a man in his seventies. In a wooded area near Mineral, Washington, Thompson noticed a landed flying saucer with naked children playing on its steps. As he approached the craft, he was greeted by naked adults. He remained with them three days and even bunked in their ship. They recounted to him that earth people and Venusians were once united, even sharing the same religion, until sin separated them. The objective of the Venusians was to slowly establish peace by contacting earth people one at a time. This will result in the return of Jesus Christ.

Can you imagine taking a stroll through the woods and stumbling across a huge spacecraft with forty-five naked men, women, and children in and around it, who tell you they are from the planet Venus? (*Next stop . . . the Twilight Zone?*) Did Samuel Thompson believe he met a commune of outer space descendants of Adam and Eve? Was this peculiar spot in the woods a simulated modern day Garden of Eden?

This story may seem totally preposterous to you, yet the UFO phenomenon is interspersed with ridiculous circumstances. This fact tends to cast the phenomenon in a negative light to the "educated" public. Is this an intentional UFO smoke screen?

In 1950 the possibility of life on Venus existed in our scientific mind. Interestingly, however, today scientists affirm that there is no life on Venus. Why, then, are these beings lying to us? Where do they really come from? They evidently wanted Samuel Thompson to think that they were from Venus.

The Adamski Puzzle

On 20 November 1952 in the Mojave Desert of California, George Adamski (b. 17 April 1891 Poland; d. 23 April 1965 near Washington D.C.) purportedly met a being named Orthon, who also claimed he was from the planet Venus. Orthon apparently communicated a message of peace and love. Orthon's physical characteristics bear a striking resemblance to religious paintings of Jesus Christ.

Oddly enough, Adamski became a celebrity, toured the world, and was publicly acknowledged as the first *contactee.* (A contactee is a person who claims to have recurring telepathic and/or physical contacts of a friendly nature with outer space beings). Adamski's renown extends to virtually every book written on UFOs. Curiously, an etymological derivation of his name appears in the Old Testament book of Genesis. Adam was the first man created by God, and *Adam*ski was the first publicly recognized contactee.

Adamski also had a most unusual birthmark. In the place of a normal naval was a pictogram of the sun. It consisted of lines extending out from around a huge circle. It covered the area from his waist to his groin. Was George Adamski's birth normal? Is there, in fact, a connection between the entities from outer space and Adamski's birth? He was evidently singled out to be one of the most controversial yet influential figures in UFO history. Did Adamski's presence set the stage for future alien activities? Was he a prominent social figure in some larger, mischievous alien plan?

On 31 May 1963 Adamski and Pope John XXIII supposedly had a secret meeting at the Vatican in Rome. Was a coming cataclysmic event discussed that will shake the entire world?

In 1965, after Adamski's death, his daughter Alice K. Wells (d. 1980) established the George Adamski Foundation in Vista, California (Wells was with Adamski on his 20 November encounter, but did not get to meet Orthon). The Foundation, now headed by Fred Steckling, comprises several thousand members worldwide with representatives in Argentina, Belgium, Denmark, England, France, Japan, Mexico, and Yugoslavia. This organization claims to receive messages from various outer space entities. These messages are published in the quarterly *Cosmic Bulletin.*

One wet Wednesday afternoon on 11 June 1980 in the small town of Todmorden, West Yorkshire, England, police officer Alan Godfrey investigated the dead body of a man discovered on top of a coal pile. Unusual burn marks were found on his head, neck, and shoulders with an oily substance of unknown origin. He had been missing since June 6. Zigmund Jan *Adamski* was his name. His bizarre disappearance and cause of death remain a mystery to this day. Strangely enough, there were numerous UFO reports in and around the town of Todmorden between 6 June and 11 June.

About five and a half months later on 28 November, less than a mile from where Adamski's body had been discovered, a UFO nearly collided with Godfrey's police car. Under hypnotic regression, it was revealed that Godfrey was taken on board the spacecraft and given some sort of medical examination.

Dr. Who?

Medical examinations performed on humans by alien beings are a common occurrence. Almost all abductees (people who are taken on board spaceships by alien beings against their will) go through some kind of medical examination inside a spacecraft (or at least they *think* they are inside a spacecraft). In some cases, individuals experience frequent abductions which often begin sometime in childhood between the ages of four and seven. A large percentage of these abductions may occur within the same family (Jacobs 1992).

The decades of the fifties, sixties, and seventies witnessed the majority of secret abductions. During these years, contactees claimed physical and telepathic contact with benevolent space people. Today, abductions and contacts continue at an alarming rate. It is estimated that over one million abductees reside in the United States, and strong evidence points to this being a worldwide phenomenon (Jacobs 1992). What is happening to these people? Are aliens manipulating the minds of everyone they abduct and, in so doing, propagating a belief in some wishful delusion?

One focus is on the breeding of children. Numerous reports indicate that sperm and eggs are extracted and used to produce alien/human offspring. The aliens convey to the abductees that these babies are the children of the future (Jacobs 1992).

Movie Magic

Abductees are often corralled together in special viewing rooms where movie-like screens depict beautiful landscapes of some futuristic new world. It would seem that this new world is being prepared for these hybrid children. It is instilled in the minds of the abductees that this is the future of *our* world. Are millions of people being brainwashed in preparation for a mass appearance of visitors from outer space?

One Step Beyond

Are these beings actually coming from another planet, or planets, in our galaxy or from some other distant galaxy? The majority of evidence says *no.* But apparently this is what they want us to *think.* It is believed that their "universe" and our universe coexist in the same physical space. These have often been referred to as other dimensions or other realities. There are key geographical locations that serve as portals or gateways where these "beings" commonly enter and exit and toy with humanity. Is the cosmic intervention that has plagued us for the past fifty years or so culminating into some fantastic near-future event? Will this event signal the beginning of the dreaded Apocalypse, as foretold in the Bible's prophetic book of Revelation?

We are now living (or trying to survive) in what most people call a glorious "New Age." Astrologers refer to this as entering a "New Great Month" in which the earth passes through a different sign of the Zodiac approximately every two thousand years. We are about to leave the Piscean Age (birth of

Christ to A.D. 2000) and enter into the Age of Aquarius.

Mary Appears

During the Age of Pisces, which is symbolized by the fish, humanity was significantly influenced by the birth of Christ and the inauguration of Christianity. Additionally, an endless number of Marian apparitions have been documented by the Catholic church since 1531 in thirty-two countries. For centuries, people throughout the world have reported seeing manifestations of the Blessed Virgin Mary. Remarkably, these manifestations often occur consecutively on the thirteenth of each month (i.e., Fatima, Portugal: 13 May 1917 to 13 October 1917).

The reported number of Marian apparitions has risen dramatically throughout the world since the 1960s; in the following years, whence the Vatican has reported more than two hundred accounts annually. Mexico, Guatemala, Puerto Rico, Venezuela, Ecuador, Argentina, France, Ireland, Spain, Portugal, Lebanon, the Philippines, Israel, Italy, Belgium, Egypt, Yugoslavia, Japan, Ukraine, Rwanda, Australia, South Korea, and the United States have all experienced some type of Marian apparition during the Piscean Age.

By 1994 the United States was host to Marian apparitions in Conyers, Georgia (Nancy Fowler, 13th of each month); Hollywood, Florida (Rosa Lopez, 13th of each month); Belleville, Illinois (Ray Doiron, 13th of each month); Lubbock, Texas (Mary Constancio); Phoenix, Arizona (Estela Ruiz, the first Saturday of every month since 3 December 1988); Bayside, Queens, N.Y. (Veronica Lueken since 7 April 1970); Cold Spring, Kentucky; Seven Hills, Ohio;

New Orleans; Marlboro Township, N.J.; Santa Ana, California; and numerous other locations.

These miraculous events rally millions of people to these various sites around the globe, with some traveling thousands of miles. Several examples may be cited: 13 October 1994: more than twenty-three thousand people amassed in Conyers, Georgia; 31 August 1994: eight thousand showed up in Cold Spring, Kentucky; 15 August 1988: fifteen thousand reportedly congregated in Lubbock, Texas. Of particular note here is that in 1951 on several different nights in August, September, and October, multiple UFO lights flying in a V-formation were observed by dozens of people over Lubbock, Texas, known as the "Lubbock Lights." Additionally, in Levelland, Texas (approximately thirty miles due west of Lubbock), on the night of 2 November 1957 there was a series of extraordinary UFO sightings by fifteen individuals.

Marian apparitions are usually accompanied by miraculous healings and specific messages from Christ. These messages often contain similar warnings: turn our hearts toward God or there will be much suffering from flood, famine, war, and other afflictions.

The phenomenon appears to center around one individual who witnesses these manifestations and repeatedly communicates with the Virgin Mary. This person acts as a conduit who passes these heavenly messages on to the multitudes gathered. Groups of children are sometimes involved, as in the case of the apparitions of Fatima, Portugal, in 1917 and those of Medjugorje, Bosnia (Yugoslavia), from 1981 to the present.

These manifestations sometimes include paranormal phenomena such as unusual brilliant or spinning lights and spinning crosses. Are these manifestations of the Virgin Mary reinforcing the principles of Christianity to certain populations? Are they a symbolic warning of the dawning of the Age of Aquarius?

When the Moon Is In the Seventh House . . .

The Age of Aquarius *is* upon us. Science and technology virtually rule society, completely overlooking the actual needs of humanity. Despite these technological achievements, thousands still die from hunger, war, and disease.

Between 1963 and 1969, a rare alignment occurred in the sign of Virgo between the two planets Uranus and Pluto. Some astrologers believe that people born between these years will have a widespread influence on humanity as we enter the Aquarian age. These individuals will either exert a positive influence (the hope of humanity) or a negative influence (the destruction of the world).

Interestingly enough, a rare alignment of planets occurred on 5 February 1962, the alleged birthdate of the anti-Christ in the Middle East, and certain astrologers predicted the end of the world. Will this "anti-Christ" emerge as a political or religious figure (or both?) as we enter this Age of Aquarius? Is this individual connected with the UFO phenomenon? Has this "anti-Christ" been a contactee since childhood?

Psychic Supermarket

A cosmic intelligence has been in contact with Uri Geller since his psychic abilities became evident at the age of three. He has since demonstrated his psychokinetic and telepathic powers throughout the world. Geller, who was born in Tel Aviv, Israel, 20 December 1946, claims that he has even received predictions regarding mass landings of UFOs.

Today the world is full of people claiming psychic abilities. There are even psychic hotlines that may be called for a price. Just turn on your television and be dazzled by astonishing psychic predictions (usually pertaining to love, money, and health). After all, everyone wants to know what their future holds. So, what is in store for humanity's future?

The Truth Shall Set You Free

Something unimaginable is going on that involves our entire planet, and hardly anyone realizes it. Most of us are too busy trying to make a living, raise a family, or get an education to recognize its mechanism. We can only see what is on the surface because that is all we are supposed to see. We assume that we are getting all of the facts when, in actuality, what we are seeing and hearing is only a glimpse of what is really going on. We are, however, being conditioned to think a certain way and to accept certain beliefs, but this is a process that takes time. This phenomenon is targeting everyone, especially the children, and it is affecting millions globally.

UFOs, UFO contacts, alien abductions, animal mutilations, crop circles, some visions of the Blessed Virgin Mary, psychic phenomena, the supernatural, religion, the occult, numerology, astrology, science, politics, the United States government, the United States military, television, and certain key individuals (along with the general public) are collectively instrumental in its sinister plan.

We can learn from the experiences of others who have already been involved in this extraordinary UFO phenomenon. However, we must keep an open mind and not discount anything that has already happened. We must also remember that, in some cases, what is really significant is the overall effect or influence a particular incident has on people, rather than the incident itself.

The New Testament of the Bible further enlightens us on this otherworldly dimension:

> Finally, my brethren, be strong in the Lord, and in the power of his might. Put on the whole armour of God, that ye may be able to stand against the wiles of the devil. For we wrestle not against flesh and blood, but against principalities, against powers, against the rulers of the darkness of this world, against spiritual wickedness in high places. (Eph. 6:10-12)

> Then if any man shall say unto you, "Lo, here is Christ, or there;" believe it not. For there shall arise false christs, and false prophets, and shall shew great signs and wonders; insomuch that, if it were possible, they shall deceive the very elect. Behold, I have told you before. Wherefore if they shall say unto you, "Behold, he is in the desert;" go not forth: "behold, he is in the secret chambers;" believe it not. (Matt. 24:23-26)

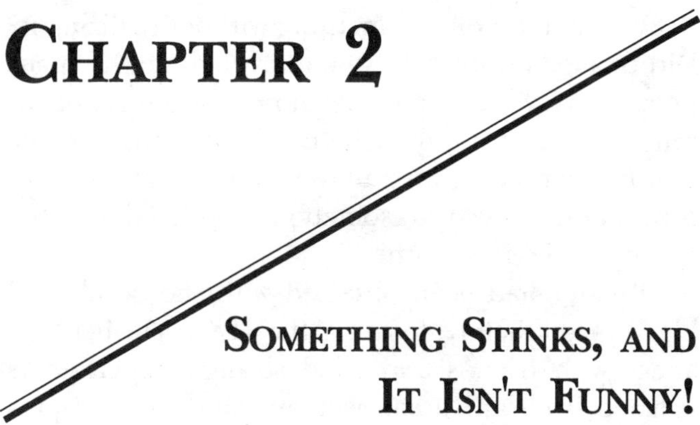

Chapter 2

Something Stinks, and It Isn't Funny!

Albert K. Bender

On 15 March (the *ides* of March) 1953 the International Flying Saucer Bureau, an organization formed in April 1952, by Albert K. Bender (born 1921) of Bridgeport, Connecticut, decided to conduct an experiment called "World Contact Day." This experiment involved hundreds of IFSB members throughout the United States, Canada, Great Britain, France, Australia, and New Zealand. All members were instructed to participate by memorizing a specific message and then simultaneously send it telepathically to outer space beings.

At precisely six P.M. eastern standard time, Bender, along with hundreds of participants, began projecting the message. After sending it three times, an alien voice responded by communicating with Bender's mind and commanded him to discontinue his investigative activities. That same year Bender mysteriously and abruptly shut down the IFSB after several frightening visits from three strange men dressed in black who materialized and dematerialized inside Bender's home.

Was Bender onto something without realizing it? Did this experiment, in some way, agitate the space people? With such an enormous concentration of mind power directed at these "aliens," it is possible that Bender, along with all the members of the IFSB throughout the world, somehow interfered with the space people's telepathic frequencies.

Bender had been obsessed with the occult and black magic before forming the IFSB. He held seances with friends and tried strange experiments learned from an Indian woman. One of his rooms became a "chamber of horrors." Bender painted grotesque images on the walls and displayed skulls, spiders and shrunken heads on his shelves. Even at an early age his family informed him that certain relatives were mysteriously involved with the supernatural (Bender 1962). Can a connection be made between Bender's dabbling in the occult and his flying saucer investigations?

Sometime after Bender began his flying saucer investigations, he was plagued by 12 strange and terrifying encounters. For years his life was in jeopardy. During and after his extraordinary encounters with alien beings, he suffered severe headaches as well as pains over his eyes. These pains were always located in the exact spot the alien's staring eyes penetrated him. For the rest of his life, he feared the reoccurrence of these headaches (Bender 1962). Did Bender suffer permanent damage as a result of his bizarre incidents with alien beings?

The John Stuart Connection

Bender's experiences may be paralleled to the late John Stuart and Doreen Wilkinson, UFO researchers from Hamilton, New Zealand, for whom the year 1954 became a year of terror, horror, and fear. They were confronted by a green, evil, hideous monster, and were subsequently warned by the monster to cease their UFO investigations. It is interesting to note that Bender also spoke of seeing a hideous monster depicted on a screen in some sort of viewing room.

Wilkinson reportedly was raped by an invisible entity and bare scratches over her whole body. Stuart was visited by an "evil thing," vaguely resembling a human. From the waist up it was a man; from the waist down it was a woman. It spoke to Stuart telepathically, warning him to cease his research. To his shock and amazement, the male and female halves switched places. After warning Stuart a second time, it dissolved into thin air (Stuart 1963). Finally in December 1954, as a result of their horrendous experiences, Stuart and Wilkinson halted all research.

As was the case with Bender, Stuart also delved into the hidden realm of the occult. Immersing himself in occult subjects including spiritualism and black magic, he surmised that *Satan* may, in fact, lie behind the UFO mystery. Was Stuart on the verge of discovering the real force behind the UFO phenomenon?

Six important similarities discovered between Al Bender and John Stuart are as follows:

1. Their UFO research began in the early 1950s (1952-1954).

2. They both exhibited an interest in the occult.

3. Each encountered a hideous monster.

4. They both experienced powerful intimidation by the phenomenon's various manifestations, leading them to abruptly cease their UFO research.

5. Materializations were accompanied by a suffocating, nauseous *odor.*

6. They both communicated with Gray Barker (1925—1984).

Gray Barker Spreads the News

Gray Barker, a lifelong resident of West Virginia, became involved with the UFO phenomenon in the early fifties. One early, unforgettable experience was his investigation of the "Flatwoods monster" case. On 12 September 1952 in Flatwoods, West Virginia, eight people (two adults and six children) witnessed a huge, frightening creature with glowing eyes while they were investigating the landing of an unidentified bright red object on a nearby hill. There was an unusual mist over the ground along with a sickly, irritating odor.

Barker joined the IFSB in 1952. He later founded Saucerian Press and published Bender's book, *Flying Saucers and the Three Men*, in 1962. In 1963 he published Stuart's book, *UFO Warning*.

One month prior to the "Flatwoods" incident, on 19 August 1952 near West Palm Beach, Florida, J.D. "Sonny" Desvergers witnessed the landing of an unidentified object. While investigating the phenomenon on foot, he came across a frightening, hideous monster. This creature emitted a peculiar "ray" which quickly paralyzed him. The area smelled worse than rotten eggs and nearly suffocated him.

The Significant Years: 1952-1954

Following is a chronological sequence of significant UFO events that occurred between 1952 and 1954. This list highlights certain individuals who have been contacted by various outer space entities, as well as ten of the major UFO sightings. (Note: there were thousands of UFO sightings reported throughout the world between 1952 and 1954, including a "flap" [heavy concentration] in the United States in July 1952. Incidentally, in 1952, over 1,500 UFO sightings were reported in the U.S. Additionally, in September and October 1952, another "flap" occurred in Europe.)

1. 6 January 1952 (Mojave Desert, California): Contactee George W. Van Tassel (1910—1978) initially receives telepathic messages from more than twenty different outer space entities, including Ashtar. Alphabetically, nineteen of these entities are: Ashtar, Clatu, Clota, Elcar, Hulda, Kerrull, Lata, Latamarx, Leektow, Locktopar, Lutbunn, Luu, Molca, Noma, Oblow, Portla, Singba, Solganda, and Totalmon (the alphabetical significance will be elaborated on later).
2. April 1952 (Bridgeport, Connecticut): The International Flying Saucer Bureau is formed (IFSB).
3. 24 May 1952 (Burbank, California): Contactee Orfeo Matthew Angelucci (born 1912 New Jersey-?, now deceased), after seeing a UFO, has his first telepathic contact with outer space entities. An alien voice orders him to drink a delicious beverage from a "crystal cup" that mysteriously materializes in front of him.
4. 18 July 1952 (Mojave Desert, California): George Van Tassel channels the first psychic messages from Ashtar. Subsequently, telepathic contact with the "Ashtar Command" occurs regularly in the years to follow.
5. 19-20 July 1952 (Washington, D.C.): Multiple sightings of UFOs are reported.

6. 23 July 1952 (California ?): Angelucci enters a strange spherical object where he then has a second telepathic encounter with entities from outer space.
7. 26-27 July 1952 (Washington, D.C.): Multiple sightings of UFOs are reported.
8. July 1952 (Nevada desert): Contactee Truman Bethurum (1898—1969) has his first contact (physical) with space people who inform him they are from the planet Clarion, a planet in our solar system hidden by the moon. Aura Rhanes, a gorgeous spacewoman and captain of the spaceship, becomes Bethurum's primary contact.
9. 2 August 1952 (California): Angelucci has his first physical contact with space people.
10. 2 August—1 November 1952 (Prescott and Winslow, Arizona): George Hunt Williamson (1926—1986) and his wife Betty, together with Alfred and Betty Bailey, receive messages from over twenty different outer space intelligences via automatic writing, ouija board, and International Morse Code on a ham radio. In particular, on 12 October a strong, foul odor was present at Al Bailey's house in Winslow. Alphabetically, twenty-three of these entities are: Actar, Adu, Affa, Ankar-22, Elex, Garr, Kadar Lacu, Lomec, Nah-9, Noro, Oara, Ponnar, Regga, Ro, Sedat, Suttku, Terra, Touka, Um, Wan-4, Zago, Zo, and Zrs.
11. 19 August 1952 (Florida): Desvergers, after witnessing a landed UFO, has face to face encounter with a hideous monster. A suffocating, nauseous odor is also present.
12. 12 September 1952 (Flatwoods, West Virginia): Eight people witness the "Flatwoods

monster." A suffocating, nauseous odor is present.

13. 13-21 September 1952 (Denmark and Norway): During "Operation Mainbrace," involving eighty thousand men, military personnel report a series of astonishing UFO sightings.
14. 21 September 1952 (Morocco, Africa): Numerous UFO sightings are reported. One spectacular event is a UFO witnessed by five thousand people attending a boxing match in Casablanca.
15. 17 October 1952 (Oloron, France): Hundreds of people witness an unusually shaped, slow moving cloud. Above the cloud is a white cylindrical object tilted at a 45 degree angle. In front of the cylinder the people notice about thirty red spheres encircled by yellow rings. Mass quantities of angels' hair are seen descending toward the earth from its path.
16. 27 October 1952 (Gaillac, France): Nearly a hundred people witness a replay of the Oloron event that took place ten days earlier.
17. Circa fall, 1952 (Bridgeport, Connecticut): Desvergers' Florida encounter is reported in *Space Review*, a magazine published by Al Bender's IFSB (*Space Review* was first published in October 1952.)
18. 20 November 1952 (Desert Center, California): Contactee George Adamski's alleged notorious encounter with Orthon of Venus. (Note: accompanying Adamski on this legendary day are George and Betty Williamson, Alfred and Betty Bailey, Mrs. Alice K. Wells, and Mrs. Lucy McGinnis, Adamski's secretary.)
19. Early 1953 (Giant Rock, between Lucerne Valley and Twenty-nine Palms, California):

Van Tassel begins a regular Saturday night Spacecraft Convention, which includes *channeling* sessions and lectures from other contactees. These meetings continue until 1977. During their heyday in the 1950s, some ten thousand fans, anticipating hearing the "intergalactic gospel" of the space people, gathered at these conventions. Contactees such as George Adamski, Wayne Sulo Aho, Orfeo Matthew Angelucci, Truman Bethurum, Daniel William Fry, Gabriel Green, and George Hunt Williamson were all regular participants at these events.

20. February, 1953: Barker is appointed chief investigator for the IFSB.
21. 15 March (the *Ides* of March) 1953: IFSB's "World Contact Day."
22. July 1953 (Bridgeport, Connecticut): Bender is transported to an unknown circular room. He is forced to view a hideous monster depicted on a television-like screen. This alien creature then informs him that this is their natural appearance. Bender notices a distinct similarity between this hideous monster and the "Flatwoods monster." (Note: all of Bender's encounters were accompanied by a strange odor, similar to burning sulfur or rotten eggs.)
23. 24 August 1953 (Mojave Desert, California): Van Tassel is taken for a ride in a flying saucer by a spaceman named Solganda.
24. *Halloween*, 31 October 1953 (Eliot, Maine): Contactee Frances Swan has a "peculiar" incident with a "stranger." This stranger's identity is later revealed in communications to

Swan to be none other than Affa, an entity claiming to be from Uranus.

25. 1953 (Westchester, California): Contactee Gloria Lee (1925-1962) receives telepathic messages from "J.W.," an entity who claims to reside on Jupiter.
26. March, 1954 (London, England): Contactee George King (born 23 January 1919 in Wellington, England) receives an *audible* message that he will become the voice of "Interplanetary Parliament."
27. 30 April 1954 (Eliot, Maine): Frances Swan receives her first message from outer space via automatic writing.
28. 3 May 1954 (Eliot, Maine): Frances Swan is contacted by Affa via automatic writing. She is also contacted by Alomar from Mercury and Ponnar of Pluto.
29. June-October 1954 (Hamilton, New Zealand): John Stuart and Doreen Wilkinson are confronted by hideous creatures not long after discussing Al Bender's experiences (Stuart learned of Bender's experiences through letters from Gray Barker). Strange, nauseating odors also accompanied these materializations.
30. 28 July 1954 (Eliot, Maine): Canadian ufologist and government engineer Wilbert B. Smith (1910-1962) meets with Frances Swan in an attempt to communicate with the space beings Affa and Alomar.
31. 17 September 1954 (Rome, Italy): Thousands of people witness a spectacular UFO sighting.
32. 18 September 1954 (New Mexico and Colorado): Several thousand people witness an enormous, slow-moving green fireball.

33. 28 October 1954 (Rome, Italy): Dozens witness a UFO spewing angels' hair from its path.
34. 20 December 1954 (Chicago, Illinois): *"The end of the world!"* This public announcement is made by the late *psychic* channeler Dorothy Martin, who, prior to this date, had been receiving messages via automatic writing from an entity named Sananda. She is instructed by Sananda to make this public announcement that the world is going to end on 20 December 1954. Martin and her followers are assured they would be rescued by a flying saucer.
35. 1954 (Mojave desert, California): Carl Arthur Anderson (born 9 November 1912 in Wellfleet, Massachusetts) and his family are paralyzed for about fifteen minutes by a beam of light coming from a landed flying saucer.
36. 1954 (Merlin, Oregon): Contactee Daniel Fry's second telepathic communication with a spaceman named A-lan. (Note: the first contact occurred in 1950 on *Independence Day* (4 July) near the White Sands Proving Ground in New Mexico.)

Between 1952 and 1954, as the preceding documentation shows, the UFO phenomenon exploded into earth-shaking worldwide events. Millions of people around the globe witnessed a variety of extraordinary objects in the skies. The recurrence of major UFO events in specific geographic areas is certainly no coincidence. In fact, it is intentional. The goal is to instill in our minds that we are being visited by an advanced extraterrestrial civilization. A universal *conditioning* is taking place, masterminded by these "aliens."

The UFO phenomenon methodically targeted certain individuals. Albert K. Bender, John Stuart, Doreen Wilkinson, Gray Barker, J.D. "Sonny" Desvergers, and the eight witnesses of the Flatwoods case were all recipients of the evil and multifaceted, monstrous, malodorous phenomenal manifestations. (Barker was indirectly involved; he did not see any monsters.)

The Nose Knows

During spiritualist seances, mysterious fragrances are often detected when a "spirit" is present. In occult lore, pungent, putrid odors often accompany the materialization of an *evil* spirit. Pleasing odors (i.e., perfume, violets, or fine incense) seem to accompany *holy* people. Of particular note are stigmatics whose open wounds emit a strong pleasant fragrance. (Stigmatics are people whose skin erupts with wounds similar to those of Christ's crucifixion on the cross.)

A careful investigation of these ongoing events reveals an obvious connection between the UFO phenomenon and the occult. In the 1950s it was ludicrous to think that black magic (or Satanism), along with hideous monsters that smell like hydrogen sulfide, were tied in with flying saucers.

Shifting Focus

Today, even though the bizarre and supernatural continue to surround numerous UFO incidents, people still refuse to accept it. UFO researchers have a tendency to focus their attention and efforts on exposing supposed U.S. government cover-ups of alleged crashed saucers and alien autopsies; Roswell, New Mexico is a case in point (July 1947). Roswell, and the whole idea of crashed saucers, is leading good researchers on a wild goose chase and the general public astray. The impression left in the human mind is constantly being fueled by fabricated evidence.

The U.S. government *is* intricately involved with the UFO phenomenon, but not in the way we have been led to believe it is. The government is using the UFO phenomenon deceptively on humanity, and, in so doing, masquerading its own ulterior motives. The government's main objective is to lure us away from actual covert activities, in an attempt to propagate an erroneous belief system. Likewise, the intelligence behind the UFO phenomenon is using the U.S. government and other organizations and individuals for *its* own ulterior motives.

So, in reality, we have deception upon deception on a massive scale. This, in turn, makes uncovering the actual truth extremely complex. Every attempt at untangling this web of confusion leads to a mixed bag of veritable possibilities. Hence, we have a multitude of divergent theories regarding UFOs and their occupants.

The "O" Cult

In the last fifty years we have seen in our society a revival in the Occult Sciences (or the Hermetic Sciences). Occultism is the belief that one is able to use or control supernatural powers mysteriously hidden from humans. Occultists usually operate secretly and often disguise subversive activities. The practice of magic is essential and may incorporate a secret Satanic theology that misuses latent human psychic abilities. Communication with supernatural beings is common.

Satanists, whose sects are scattered throughout the world, employ theurgy (a branch of *operative* magic), which involves the practice of certain magical rites that evoke supernatural beings and direct them to earth.

Secret societies, such as occultists, Satanists, modern day psychics, channelers, and trance mediums, who summon supernatural beings are, in actuality, using and controlling inexplicable forces. Such unorthodox groups are, in fact, reinforcing the intentions and enhancing the primary goals of these supernatural entities (either knowingly or unknowingly) by repeated invocations.

We have provided these entities, who already exert unlimited physical and psychic power over us, with a wide open door into our reality. But are we able to restrict these compelling creatures whom we have welcomed with open arms? Or are they roaming freely, seeking whom they may devour? Might these occultists be summoning Ashtar?

CHAPTER 3

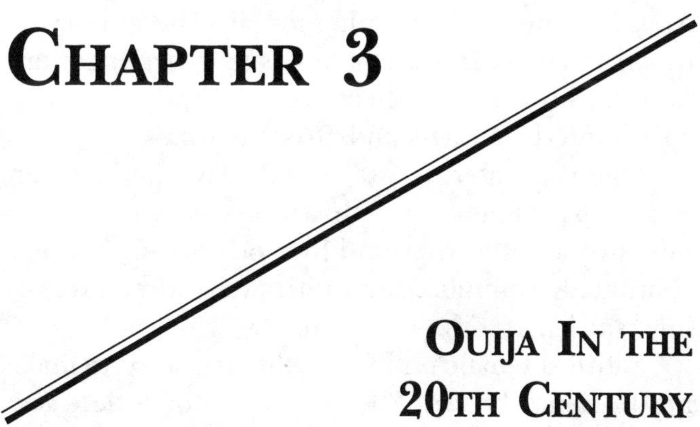

OUIJA IN THE 20TH CENTURY

The Gulf Breeze Six

In the mid-1980s Vance A. Davis, who throughout his life evidenced *psychic* abilities, joined the U.S. Army. He attended the Military Occupational Specialty School in Pensacola, Florida (about five miles northwest of Gulf Breeze), where he eventually met Ken Beason. They became good friends after realizing they shared similar *science fiction* interests.

During the summer of 1989, Davis and Beason were stationed in Augsburg, Germany. They began delving into Tarot cards, hypnosis, pendulums, and deep meditation. Later that summer they decided to help Beason's girlfriend Alex, who had been terrorized by the presence of a supernatural being in her dreams. Davis, while in a meditative state, entered into some kind of "spiritual realm" where, remarkably, he was confronted by a huge claw-like monster with blood-red eyes approaching Alex's body. Davis immediately called upon Jesus Christ in an effort to protect Alex. Suddenly a bright light surrounded Alex's body. This "light" attacked the horrible creature, which then vanished into thin air. Since then

Alex has never been plagued by these horrific dreams. These and other fantastic experiences are fully documented in their book *Unbroken Promises,* co-authored by Davis and Brian Blashaw.

One year later, in May 1990, Davis and Beason began experimenting with a ouija board. For the next two months, they and four other army buddies continually communicated with twelve very interesting "spirits."

Safire, a female entity, was the first spirit to make her presence known. She claimed to be a deceased earthling named Velda who passed away in the 1960s and supposedly resided in Sebina, Georgia. Baqraun, a Tibetan monk from the twelfth century, also revealed himself through the ouija. Another was "Nostro," who they all perceived to be the sixteenth century clairvoyant Nostradamus (1503-1566). The remaining nine spirits were particularly significant characters from the Bible: Mary (the mother of Jesus), Timothy, Matthew, Mark, Luke, John, Paul, Simon (or Peter), and Zacharias. Some of these biblical entities referred to themselves as the "Guardians."

All in all there were seven sessions with the ouija board. Davis, Beason, and their four friends were given specific predictions and messages regarding humanity's future. The following is a list of these messages:

1. The world is very close to the time of the tribulation that is prophesied in the Bible.
2. During the decade of the 1990s, the U.S. government will be replaced by the New World Order.
3. The bankruptcy of the United States will result in a changeover of the world's central power to the United Nations of Europe.

4. The decline of the U.S. economy will trigger the emergence of a national police force.
5. The creation of a single world currency will be followed by the formation of a world government.
6. The "anti-Christ" is currently roaming about in and among political powers. His rise to power out of Europe is imminent. In 1998 he will reveal to the world that he is "the Messiah." He also claims leadership of both the European Council and a new world council.

These six individuals truly believe they were communicating with actual personages from the Bible. In so doing, they accepted the fact that they indeed were a "chosen" group. The aforementioned biblical entities directed them to embark on a special "mission" whose objective was to awaken the population of the United States to this precognitive "gospel truth." Their first order of business was to make Americans aware of the specific political and economic changes about to occur in the near future. People needed to understand why these imminent changes were going to take place. This mission also included an assignment requiring them to assist *children* as well as adults during the Tribulation's turbulent times.

Not even two months later, on 6 July 1990 in an attempt to fulfill the prophecies that were transmitted to them by means of the ouija board, these six individuals went AWOL en route to Gulf Breeze, Florida. Eventually they were arrested in Gulf Breeze and subsequently imprisoned at Fort Knox. An interrogation took place with certain government officials, but three weeks later they were set free.

During the few weeks in which they were being guarded, the media got wind of the situation and began publicizing various interpretations of this incredible series of circumstances. These wild stories, however, revealed the following information:

1. These six army deserters were now referred to as the "Gulf Breeze Six."
2. They were labeled cult members belonging to a group known as "The End of the World."
3. They arrived in Gulf Breeze with a motive to kill the "anti-Christ."
4. They were also in Gulf Breeze to meet with an unidentified UFO author in an attempt to expose the U.S. government's cover-up of alien intervention that is now taking place on earth.

A Voice In the Wind

Prior to this "Gulf Breeze Six" hoopla, another central figure had emerged. Ed Walters gained notoriety through an amazing sequence of UFO sightings occurring in Gulf Breeze between 11 November 1987 and 1 May 1988. Additionally, more than one hundred people also reported seeing similar objects. Walters managed to snap thirty-nine photographs of these circular, luminous objects using five different types of cameras. His experiences were published in 1990 in the book *The Gulf Breeze Sightings*, co-authored with his wife.

During his UFO sightings, Walters often heard male and female voices in his head that sometimes spoke in Spanish (he did live for a short while in Central America). These voices, however, frequently sounded distorted or computer-like. They addressed him as "Zehaas" and repeated the phrase "twelve wait." He soon encountered strange beings in and around his home. In June 1988 Walters submitted to a series of hypnotic regression sessions which revealed that numerous alien abductions had taken place in his life (Walters and Walters 1994).

It is interesting to note that the "Gulf Breeze Six" were arrested at the home of a friend and schoolmate of Ed Walters' daughter. The media cashed in on this connection, and they spawned a series of articles attempting to tie Walters' UFO experiences to the "Gulf Breeze Six." Some reporters even speculated that Walters had somehow been in contact with these six army deserters. The clincher was that there were actually reporters who wanted to know if Ed Walters was indeed the "anti-Christ."

Did the news media unconsciously stumble on a grandiose scheme? Was it just a coincidence that the eccentric activities of the "Gulf Breeze Six" were, in fact, connected to the UFO claims of Ed Walters? Or were they all pawns in a master-minded plot? If so, why? By whom? Apparently, when the decade of the 1990s began, the "anti-Christ" became associated with the UFO phenomenon.

Six members of the U.S. military had received startling predictions from so-called biblical entities through a ouija board regarding the demise of the U.S. government. Was this a coincidence? Did they really communicate with Saint Paul and Saint Peter? After all, the messages they received can be traced, in part, to biblical prophecies concerning the end times. Could they, in reality, have been in contact with ethereal impostors? Does the phrase "twelve wait" (instilled in Ed Walters' mind by "alien" beings) have any connection to the twelve "spirits" Davis and his fellow soldiers communicated with during their seven sessions with the ouija?

Open Sesame

The ouija consists of a board that displays the words "yes" and "no," the letters of the alphabet, the numbers zero through nine, and a heart-shaped pointer. It is used frequently for clairvoyance and for contacting invisible entities or "spirits." After placing one's fingertips on the pointer and asking a question, the pointer will suddenly move (by means of an unknown force) to specific locations on the board to answer that question. Many Christians consider the ouija board to be a doorway into the realm of the *demonic.* Participants often encounter unseen forces and sometimes become possessed by *evil* spirits.

The ouija dates back to 551 B.C. when the Chinese used similar means to communicate with the dearly departed. The ancient Greeks and Romans also used divining instruments (like the ouija) to obtain revelations from the "spirit world." The planchette, an improved version of the ouija board, came into existence in Europe during the nineteenth century. It too consisted of a heart-shaped ouija pointer but had a pencil attached for direct transcription of spiritual messages onto a piece of paper.

The Pen Is Mightier...

Eventually the planchette was discarded, and "spirit" communication took place by direct means. *Automatic writing* is achieved while an individual is in a trance-like state and is holding a pen or pencil in a normal fashion. The ability to write is then imparted to the recipient by some invisible intelligence. Automatic writing is a contemporary way to make contact and communicate with unseen entities. This method is used extensively by New Agers. Unfortunately, like practitioners of the ouija, participants in automatic writing may become possessed by evil entities, commonly known as *demons.* These entities latch on to an individual and often torment them mentally and physically for years.

As early as the 1950s, contactees, namely, Gloria Lee, Frances Swan, George Hunt Williamson, and Dorothy Martin (Sister Thedra), began receiving messages from outer space beings via automatic writing. Even today automatic writing is being utilized as one method of communication with supposed alien beings aboard spaceships.

Will the Real Jesus Please Stand Up?

Dorothy Martin's name is significant because she was the leader of a flying saucer contactee group, and she communicated with an entity named Sananda via automatic writing. Sananda, also known as the Radiant One, claims to be *Jesus the Christ,* and to this day exerts influence on people devoted to New Age ideologies or UFO organizations. Representing such various space agencies as the "Intergalactic Space Confederation," the "Interplanetary Alliance and Space Commands," the "World Federation," the "Alliance of Planets," the "Free Federation of Planets," and so on, Ashtar, known as "Commander in Chief," ranks second only to Sananda, whose title "*Beloved* Commander in Chief" takes preeminence.

The Ashtar Command

Sananda has evidently given Ashtar leadership of the Ashtar Command. In 1980, on *Independence Day,* a New York businessman experienced his first channeling session with Ashtar. This began a series of thirty-five transmissions received from Ashtar and other beings involved with the Ashtar Command including Monka, Aura Raines (Rhanes), Solar Star, Romilar, and The Etherians. (As noted in chapter two, a similar series of telepathic transmissions took place in July 1952 when George Van Tassel began channeling messages from Ashtar and the Ashtar Command.)

The Ashtar Command boasts many great fleets of spaceships occupied by thousands of outer space beings. One of its missions includes the evacuation of selected human *souls* during cataclysmic events on earth. The Ashtar Command also has four associates involved in its operations including Soltec of the Scientific Patrols, Monka (Soltec's father) of the Tribunal Councils, Korton of the Communications Service, and Athena of the Starship of Sananda.

TCN: The Channeling Network

Today, at an alarming rate, these numerous noble space beings of the Ashtar Command are communicating through "special" human individuals via *channeling.* Channeling is also conducted while in a trance-like state whereby an unseen entity temporarily takes possession of the channeler's body and communicates by speaking directly through him or her. The channeler may also transmit "alien" messages via automatic writing or a ouija board. Hence, as a direct result of these transmissions, numerous books are written and published.

Interestingly enough, channeling dates back to the ancient Egyptians, Greeks, Chinese, and Babylonians who channeled communications from various "gods" or disembodied spirits.

Channeling is an integral part of the New Age movement. The current primary channeler for the Ashtar Command is Tuella (Thelma B. Terrell). Her channeled manuscripts to date include *Project World Evacuation* (1993), *Ashtar* (1994), *On Earth Assignment* (1994), *Cosmic Prophecies For the Year 2,000* (1994), and *A New Book of Revelations* (1995).

Transmission Failure

One of many outer space beings involved with the Ashtar Command who channels messages regularly through Tuella and others is Kuthumi, who holds the title World Teacher. Through his transmissions, Kuthumi dictated a carefully designed plan conceived by the Ashtar Command which parallels a particular mission to be carried out by New Age disciples.

Back in 1895 Alice LaTrobe Bateman Bailey (1880—1949) was visited by a mysterious stranger wearing a turban who informed her that she would be involved in an important mission. She perceived this stranger to be *Jesus Christ.* Then, in 1915 she visited the Theosophical Society in Pacific Grove, California. There, on the wall, she saw a picture of a Kasmirian Indian whose body supposedly was inhabited by an ascended "Tibetan master" named "Koot Hoomi." It was then she realized that Koot Hoomi was, in fact, this mysterious stranger who had visited her in 1895 when she was only fifteen. Of particular interest here is one of the prophecies of Nostradamus, where a man wearing a turban is mysteriously associated with the "anti-Christ."

An Occult Trinity

Alice Bailey, who was part of an *occult female trinity,* actually rose to prominence through the Theosophical Society. The two others were Russian mystic Madame Helena Petrovna Blavatsky (known as HPB, 1831—1891), who founded the Theosophical Society in New York in September 1875, and Annie (Wood) Besant (1847—1933), her successor. Worth noting here is the fact that Koot Hoomi, ("Master K.H."), was originally contacted by Madame Blavatsky, who claimed that in 1868 they met face to face. The revelations received by these three women have since guided the course of today's New Age movement.

A Society's Roots

The Theosophical Society is an occult organization that communicates through channeling with a group of highly intellectual Tibetan *adepts* known as the "Ascended Masters." Blavatsky also believed that a "spiritual hierarchy" of Ascended Masters existed and resided on the planet Venus. These Venusian lords were called the "Lords of the Flame." A group of lower masters, known as the "Lords of the Seven Rays," were in direct contact with Blavatsky and other "special" human beings. Today the Theosophical Society has five main locations: Adyar, Madras, India; Wheaton, Illinois; Altadena, California; Los Angeles, California; and London, England.

A Cool Character

The prolific Alice Bailey channeled nineteen books from Tibetan masters in three decades, most of which came through Djwhal Khul (or Djual Khool), one of the more important masters who contacted Bailey in November 1919. (Djwhal Khul also was originally contacted by Madame Blavatsky.) He dictated "The Plan," outlined in *The Externalization of the Hierarchy*, which is revered by leaders of the New Age movement around the globe. In fact, the present mission being carried out by New Age followers has been fueled by its revelations.

There is nothing "new" under the sun. For more than twenty years George Adamski received messages from outer space beings via psychic channeling. His famous encounter in the Mojave Desert on 20 November 1952 with Orthon of Venus was directly linked to these channeled messages. Tibetan masters apparently play a vital role in many psychic channeling occurrences. George Adamski often spoke of receiving channeled messages from certain "Tibetan masters." We would also do well to recall the case of the "Gulf Breeze Six" and their communication with Baqraun, a Tibetan monk.

Another series of channeled messages via automatic writing emerged through Gloria Lee who, in 1953, began receiving telepathic messages from *J.W.*, a spaceman from Jupiter. These messages were later published and distributed to her followers. J.W.'s teachings, which are theosophical in nature, bear a striking resemblance to Alice Bailey's channeled transmissions of D*jw*hal Khul (also known as "the Tibetan"). By comparing the two names J.W. and Djwhal Khul, we can surmise that, in all likelihood, we are dealing with the same entity. In 1962 J.W. ordered Lee to go on a fast for peace. After sixty-six days she died of starvation.

Unarius

Theosophical connections abound as in the case of Ernest L. Norman (d. 1971) and his wife Ruth Marian Norman (1900-1993). In 1954 they established the flying saucer group Unarius (Universal Articulate Inter-dimensional Understanding of Science). Ernest Norman was a spiritualist *medium* (a person who communicates with non-physical entities while in a trance-like state) who had also been involved with Borderland Sciences Research Associates (BSRA), an occult theosophical group founded by the late N. Meade Layne in Vista, California in February 1945.

Ernest, who claimed to have been *Jesus* in a past life, began receiving channeled messages from outer space beings of the "Intergalactic Confederation" who claimed residence on Mars and Venus. After the death of her husband in 1971, Ruth, who claimed to have been *Mary Magdalene* in a past life, continued the channelings along with two students who were given the names Antares and Cosmon.

In 1973 Ruth experienced a vision in which she married the archangel Michiel (the biblical archangel Michael?). She was then renamed Uriel. It should be noted here that the continuous channelings that took place included transmissions from George Adamski and Orfeo Angelucci on the planet Venus.

The following year, on 17 March 1974, the purpose of the "Intergalactic Confederation Project" was revealed to Uriel: in the year 2001, thirty-three spaceships (some as large as five miles in diameter) will land on top of one another near San Diego, California. Nearly three years later, in 1977, Unarius purchased sixty-seven acres near Jamul, California, precisely where the friendly space people of the Intergalactic Confederation had told Uriel they would land.

The Kingpin

Since 1954 another key channeler, George King, has served as the "primary terrestrial mental channel" of Cosmic Intelligences known as the "Cosmic Masters." In 1956 King, a skilled occultist, founded and presided over the Aetherius Society (a UFO contactee organization). Four of these Cosmic Masters include Aetherius (a Venusian), an entity that calls himself *Jesus Christ* (Sananda?), Mars Sector 6, and Jupiter 92.

King received numerous channeled transmissions directing him to perform certain tasks that would benefit Earth. During one particular mission, Operation Prayer Power, King gathered the spiritual energy accumulated through prayer and somehow physically contained it. Later this energy was released to prevent natural disasters. In 1958 King carried out Operation Starlight which lasted a little over three years. He was instructed by "Master *Jesus,*" who resides on the planet Venus, to spiritually charge eighteen different mountains to help keep away the forces of *evil.*

Mark My Words

Not many people realized that channeling punctuated the decade of the 1950s. One such channeler, who was briefly mentioned in chapter two, was George Hunt Williamson (also known as "Ric" Williamson), who received telepathic transmissions from so-called outer space beings via automatic writing and the ouija board. Additionally, close friends and associates of Williamson also claimed that he channeled space messages while in a trance-like state. He eventually became known by his space name Mark III. Williamson was also influenced by theosophical underpinnings in the occult doctrines of the Borderland Sciences Research Associates.

In 1956 he traveled to the Andes Mountains near Lake Titicaca, Peru and organized the Brotherhood of the Seven Rays, a metaphysical group in which Dorothy Martin served as one of its primary channelers. It was at this time that he changed his name to "Brother Philip." It is interesting to note that in 1955, prior to this trip, William Mardorf discovered the ruins of an ancient submerged city in Lake Titicaca.

Notice how the names Sananda and Kuthumi keep cropping up, particularly in relation to channeling. Another UFO contactee organization, the Universariun Foundation (co-founded by Zelrun Wallace Karsleigh, its primary channeler), receives transmissions from outer space beings and ascended masters. These include messages from Sananda and Kuthumi.

Compuserve

Today, telepathic messages are being transmitted in proportion to our technological advancements. Now UFO entities are communicating through individuals who, while in a trance-like state, record the received messages on their personal computers, the latest form of "automatic writing."

CHAPTER 4

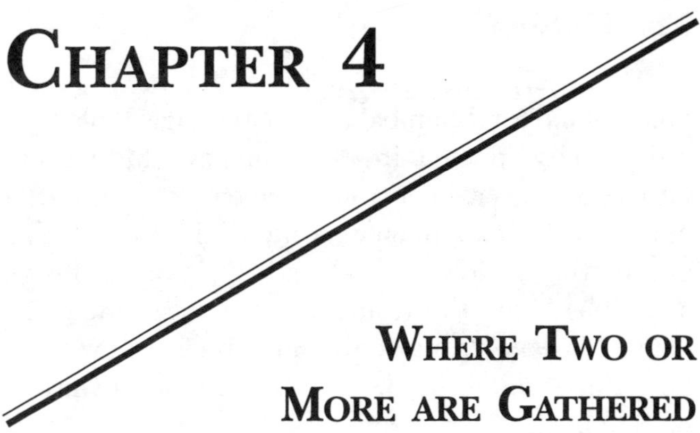

WHERE TWO OR MORE ARE GATHERED

Lord Maitreya

"THE CHRIST IS NOW HERE" appeared in a full-page ad on Sunday, 25 April 1982 in seventeen major cities throughout the world. Sponsoring this media blitz was the Tara Center, a New Age theosophical organization influenced by the work of Alice Bailey and founded in 1980 by Benjamin Creme (b. 1922, Scotland). This declaration was intended to inform all humanity that "the Christ" would appear within the next two months. Evidently, however, this spectacular "appearance" never occurred.

This New Age "Christ" apparently is a spirit entity known as Lord Maitreya who supposedly originates from the legendary mystical Tibetan kingdom Shambhala and now has manifested himself on Earth. Maitreya still claims he will reveal himself to humanity as the Christ by appearing on national television where he can simultaneously communicate his message telepathically to all people.

The Hidden City

Strangely enough, many Tibetans perceive Shambhala (or Shamballah) to be a real place, a hidden city located in the Himalaya Mountains. Others, however, believe it is only a myth. Still others think of Shambhala as a mystical kingdom that guards the world's most sacred spiritual teachings, as well as being the residence of the ascended "Tibetan Masters." Amazingly, Shambhala is even believed by some to be the site of the biblical Garden of Eden.

Creme of the Crop

The roots of the Maitreyan communiques can be traced back to 1957 when Benjamin Creme (residing in London at the time) joined George King's Aetherius Society. Here he learned to transmit spiritual powers that were received from outer space beings. Not long afterwards he discovered that he had the ability to heal.

Soon after, however, Creme left the Aetherius Society and in 1959 began receiving messages from these outer space entities (or ascended masters) concerning the *re*appearance of Maitreya. It was during this time that he became the primary channeler for Maitreya himself, and he still is to this day. In fact, the April 1982 announcement of Maitreya's appearance as "the Christ" was a direct result of channeled communications between Maitreya and Creme. Also, it is interesting to note that in 1948, one year prior to her death, Alice Bailey's channeled manuscript *The Reappearance of the Christ* revealed that the time for "the Christ" to appear was indeed approaching.

Center Stage

The Tara Center, with bases of operation in New York City; North Hollywood, California, and London, England, believes that Maitreya initially manifested himself on the earth two thousand years ago and that the real Jesus Christ was, in fact, *his* disciple. Maitreya supposedly then reappeared in 1977. Where? Shambhala? Yet the Tara Center continues to publish various newsletters and books proclaiming his existence. In so doing, the center is reviving interest in another grand reappearance. This raises a number of pertinent questions: (1) Why, in 1982, did Maitreya choose not to publicly proclaim himself as "the Christ?" (2) Could it be that the timing was not right? (3) Was this supposed "flub" an intentional smoke screen? (4) Could this whole "shebang" be, in essence, just another stepping stone in a carefully masterminded plan? (5) Is the "bang" still coming? (6) Is Maitreya's imminent reappearance affecting society today?

Maitreya Walks the Earth

According to Creme and his followers, Maitreya's "presence" has already sent shock waves that have reverberated into the world's socio-political and socio-religious systems, despite the fact that his "spectacular" appearance fell short. In August 1987, for example, Creme announced that significant changes in existing international political structures were going to take place in ensuing years as a direct result of Maitreya's presence on Earth. Since then we have witnessed such incredible events as the breakup of the Soviet Union, the unification of Germany, and the formation of a democratic government in South Africa. It should also be pointed out that in 1988,

Maitreya was photographed in Kenya and since then his picture has been circulated worldwide.

In recent years Maitreya has purportedly visited hundreds of churches and other religious organizations around the globe. Supposedly, healing properties have been miraculously added to certain water sources near these particular sites. Other "miracles" accompanying Maitreya's appearances include manifestations of the Blessed Virgin Mary, unusual brilliant crosses of light, encounters with "angelic beings," and crop circles (Melton 1996a).

Benjamin Creme's empire extends to the Share International Foundation, a subsidiary of the Tara Center. In 1981 the Foundation began publishing and distributing the magazine *Share International,* which publicizes and promotes Maitreya's "miracles." Share's headquarters are in Amsterdam, Holland, where journalist Peter Liefhebber is one of its directors. Satellite administrative offices are located in London and Los Angeles. Their objective is not only to promote Lord Maitreya as "the Christ," but to establish and help support a "New World Order."

Semantics Or "Some Antics?"

Lord Maitreya, who like Kuthumi claims the title World Teacher, is also recognized by the name "Sanat Kumara." Alice Bailey and Helena Blavatsky of the Theosophical Society both claimed that Sanat Kumara was the *supreme deity* of the "Lords of the Flame" residing on Venus. Another title of Sanat Kumara is the "Lord of this World." Today New Age leaders are proclaiming and promoting Maitreya, or Sanat Kumara, as "the Christ"

The name Sanat closely resembles Sananda (also known as *Jesus the Christ*). Notice, however, that the letters may also be rearranged to spell *Satan*. This brings us to ask five unsettling questions: (1) Is Lord Maitreya now moving about in and among religious and political institutions? (2) Could Maitreya actually be the manifestation of Satan as the anti-Christ? (3) Is Benjamin Creme really channeling messages from Satan? (4) Rather than extraterrestrials, is the Ashtar Command (Sananda's intergalactic confederacy), in fact, a legion of *demonic* beings engaged in the bidding of its commander, Satan? (5) Will the emergence of Satan as the anti-Christ (Maitreya's "grand" *re*appearance?) be heralded by a fleet of spaceships?

In February 1960, the name Kumar surfaced when Carl Anderson, an ordained minister of the International Evangelism Crusades, was taken aboard a spacecraft in the Mojave Desert. An alien named Kumar (Sanat *Kumara?*) explained the spaceship's propulsion system to him. Kumar then instructed Anderson to travel to Germany and meet with certain German engineers, including rocket scientist Hermann Oberth, and share this new revelation with them (which he did for three days).

As noted in chapter two it was six years earlier, in 1954, in the Mojave Desert, that Anderson and his family were paralyzed by a beam of light coming from a landed flying saucer. It is also worth noting that between 1954 and 1963, Kumar, who claimed he was from Massai or Mars, visited Anderson several times at his home in Fullerton, California. There Kumar often levitated and performed other miraculous feats, only to suddenly vanish into thin air. Supposedly, Anderson's last contact with Kumar took place on the night of 4 May 1963 in the Mojave Desert.

Strange Bedfellows

The organization that ordained Anderson, the International Evangelism Crusades, was founded in 1959 in Van Nuys, California. Its president and cofounder is Dr. Frank E. Stranges (born 6 October 1927). Stranges, also a minister, holds doctorates in Theology, Divinity, Psychology, Philosophy, Humanities, and Criminology and claims to have witnessed numerous UFO sightings as well as made contact with outer space beings. The Crusades boast a worldwide membership of 300,000 people with congregations in fifty countries. In the United States alone there are 125 ministers and 40 congregations. They have seminaries in Van Nuys, California, New York City, Hong Kong, South Korea, and Indonesia.

Stranges, while on an evangelical crusade in Washington, D.C. in December 1959, claimed to have met a rather unusual Venusian. Through a high ranking government official, who professed to be a born-again Christian, Stranges received a personal invitation to the Pentagon where he met Valiant Thor, a "man" who had *no fingerprints* and who maintained he was from the planet Venus. During this encounter, Thor revealed an important mission already underway that involved the mingling of certain Venusians in human affairs to help bring humanity closer to the Creator. He explained to Stranges that although he would be departing Earth on 16 March 1960, he had been active for three years with the U.S. government encouraging participation in and the formation of a one world government. Incidentally, the incredible UFO sightings that occurred over Washington, D.C. on 19 July and 20 July 1952 (noted in chapters one and two) were a direct result of Valiant Thor's orders.

Eight years after Stranges founded IEC, he founded the National Investigations Committee on UFOs (NICUFO) in 1967, also in Van Nuys, California. As president, Stranges hobnobbed with Carl Anderson and Daniel Fry, members of the Committee's U.S. National Advisory Board. Additionally, the Committee has an International Advisory Board whose foreign members reside in Canada, Puerto Rico, Hong Kong, Macau, Finland, England, West Germany, and Poland.

A Prophetess Without Honor

Parallel with Maitreya's supposed appearance on Earth, German prophetess Gabriele Wittek publicly announced in 1977 that she was receiving channeled messages from the "spirit" of "Christ." Wittek, who was born in the 1930s near Augsburg, Germany, founded the Home-bringing Mission of Jesus Christ. She also formed Spirit-of-Christ churches or "gathering places" where the public could assemble and witness *Jesus* speaking directly through her. In 1984, the Mission was replaced by Universal Life—The Inner Religion, which has propagated its teachings throughout the world. Currently, Wittek's weekly channeled transmissions are translated into ten languages and published by the organization's headquarters in Wurzburg, Germany. These booklets are distributed to Inner-Spirit-of-Christ churches in 130 cities worldwide. Universal Life has affiliates in the United States in New Haven, Connecticut; New York City; Cambridge, Massachusetts; and Aurora, Illinois. Is Gabriele Wittek channeling messages from Maitreya?

Here Comes the Sun

A term or phrase frequently communicated to channelers by supposed extraterrestrials is the *Great Central Sun* or *Great Central Mind.* New Age followers essentially equate the "Great Central Sun" with *God.* To them, it refers to the universal consciousness responsible for the evolutionary process of the human mind. The interplanetary "Great Central Sun Government," in fact, supports the Ashtar Command as revealed by Tuella's channeled manuscripts. It comes as no surprise, then, that Sanat Kumara is recognized as "the Light of the Great Central Sun" by the University of the Twelve Rays of the Grand Central Sun, an organization in Charlotte, North Carolina. They also proclaim him to be the biblical Jehovah or Yahweh (commonly known in theological circles as being derived from the tetragrammaton, or YHWH, the Hebrew covenant name of God, generally construed to mean "I am that I am").

Interestingly enough, Lord Maitreya claims to be the "Voice" of the Great Central Sun Government. His recently channeled communications with the Ashtar Command through Tuella also reveal a "Divine Plan" which is designed to initiate a "New Order."

It should be pointed out at this juncture that *Lucifer,* another name for Satan, means "light giver" and is sometimes associated with the morning or evening star, Venus. Is the term "Great Central Sun," therefore a *code,* representing Lucifer?

It's A Matter of Trust

Sanat Kumara's second coming (or Lord Maitreya, "the Christ") is also being promoted by Lucis Trust, another theosophical organization. It was founded by Alice Bailey in New York City in 1922. Prior to this, however, it existed as the Lucifer Publishing Company. (In the late 1800s Madame Blavatsky's Theosophical Society's magazine was called *Lucifer*.) Today, Lucis Trust is powerfully linked to the United Nations, with its American headquarters curiously near the United Nations Plaza in New York City. Two other headquarters are strategically placed in London, England and Geneva, Switzerland. It also has delegates in Germany and Holland.

Comprising over six thousand members worldwide, Lucis Trust's objective is to establish a "New World Order" and a "New World Religion." Six subsidiaries of this organization are: (1) the Arcane School (New York, London, and Geneva), (2) World Goodwill (New York, London, and Geneva), (3) Triangles, (4) Lucis Publishing Company, (5) Lucis Trust Libraries, and (6) Radio Lucis. These organizations were conceived by Alice Bailey as a direct result of channeled communications through Djwhal Khul and Master Kuthumi.

Serving Your Fellow Man

To help usher in this new economic One World Order and One World Religion, an occult brotherhood known as the "New Group of World Servers" has been organized by the brain trust of Lucis Trust and its affiliates. Today, these metamorphosed individuals are actively and secretly networking their plan, which has already altered our banking methods and modified our educational systems. Even our Christian belief system and our government agencies have been infiltrated by the various New Age philosophies.

The Hills Are Alive . . .

The Association of Sananda and Sanat Kumara was established in 1965 when Dorothy Martin relocated to Mount Shasta, California. Martin, prior to this, in the late 1950s changed her name to "Sister Thedra" while channeling (for a few years in South America) with George "Brother Philip" Hunt Williamson's Brotherhood of the Seven Rays. She continued to channel messages from spiritually advanced outer space beings until her recent death. Transcripts of these messages were passed on to many of her followers, who often gathered at Mount Shasta.

Mount Shasta, an inactive volcanic mountain, in recent years has become a popular haven for psychics, channelers, and followers of the New Age movement. Numerous New Age organizations have sprung up and settled there. New Agers believe that Mount Shasta's geographic location is a "power spot," or an area that contains high psychic energies. Other similar power spots have been detected across the globe where "concentrated" areas contain a strong deviation in the earth's magnetic field. Interestingly, the majority of UFO sightings occur in areas where magnetic deviations exist (Keel 1975a).

Three other major power spots in the United States are the Teton mountain range in northwest Wyoming and southeast Idaho, the Black Hills of South Dakota, and four specific areas in Sedona, Arizona. The Great Pyramids in Egypt, Stonehenge in England, Machu Picchu and the Nasca lines of Peru, Mount Fuji in Japan, and Yucatan are also recognized as power spots. Occultists consider these spots to be sacred pagan worship sites specifically chosen by ancient cultures.

A "Rockin' " Rendezvous

These power spots became the center of attention on 16-17 August 1987 when thousands of New Age disciples flocked to these peculiar locations, particularly Mount Shasta, to join together in an event known as the "Harmonic Convergence." Supposedly on these two days an astrological alignment of our nine planets occurred resulting in a peak of cosmic energy that caused a shift in the earth's "spiritual" energy. This shift is regarded by New Agers to be a turning point in the earth's evolutionary cycle.

Interestingly, at least 144,000 people had to simultaneously generate harmonious energy at these sites on these two days or else the earth would encounter a negative shift resulting in a twenty-five year period of cataclysmic changes leading to the end of the world in 2012. It was estimated that well over 144,000 people participated in this Harmonic Convergence, making it a success. The enlistment of 144,000 people to accomplish a task is not unique to New Age numerology. After all, the Bible's prophetic book of Revelation indicates that 144,000 "special" witnesses will be miraculously protected by Christ during the time of the great tribulation (cf., Rev. 7:2-8; 14:1-5).

Following this meaningful Harmonic Convergence of 1987 was to be a five year period of political and social change along with an increase in visits from "extraterrestrials." (Earlier in this chapter it was noted that in August 1987, Benjamin Creme publicly announced that Maitreya's presence on earth would make a political and religious impact on society.) New Agers now believe that another pivotal *intergalactic* Harmonic Convergence will take place in the year 2012, a significant year marked by the beginning of a new era of evolution on earth.

The Germane Foundation

Mount Shasta was also the location of a particular incident that sparked the theosophical "I Am" Religious Activity Movement that was founded in Chicago, Illinois, in the 1930s by Guy Warren Ballard (1878-1939) and his wife Edna Anne Wheeler Ballard (1886-1971).

In September of 1930 Guy Ballard, who at the time was hiking at the foot of Mount Shasta, purportedly met an individual claiming to be the legendary Saint Germain, an eighteenth century European mystic adventurer. Saint Germain, who previously had been recognized by the Theosophical Society's Helena Blavatsky as one of the Ascended Masters of the "Great White Brotherhood," appointed Ballard, his wife, and their son Donald as the sole messengers of the Great White Brotherhood. The subsequent channeled messages that they received, particularly those of Saint Germain and Master *Jesus,* further directed the teachings of the "I Am" Movement.

After inaugurating the "I Am" Religious Activity, the Ballards then organized the Saint Germain Foundation and the Saint Germain Press in 1932, which is presently located in Schaumburg, Illinois. These organizations are considered to be forerunners of the present-day New Age movement; that is demonstrated by the fact that contemporary New Age religions have adopted their theosophical teachings. Presently, Saint Germain acts as an intergalactic space being of the Solar Tribunal (and the Violet Ray), channeling his messages, which are in accordance with the transmissions of the Ashtar Command, through Tuella (and others).

A Familiar Spirit

The mysterious Saint Germain appears to be a very extraordinary character. Even though there is proof of his existence in Europe in the eighteenth century as an occultist, spy, diplomat, painter, musician, jeweler, alchemist, healer, and self-proclaimed "*god,*" there is, however, no information regarding his birth and the circumstances surrounding his presumed death are unknown. During his stay in Europe, he admitted living for centuries and even claimed that Solomon (the Old Testament biblical king) was, in fact, his acquaintance. Amazingly, numerous reports have surfaced of Count Saint Germain's appearance after his supposed death. Has Saint Germain taken on the persona we customarily attribute to a *vampire?* Are the Ascended Masters of the Great White Brotherhood immortal human beings?

The Great White Brotherhood

The Great White Brotherhood (also known as the "Mahatmas") is believed by many occultists to be a group of *godlike* "adepts" (the Ascended Masters of Blavatsky's Theosophical Society) who supposedly dwell somewhere in the Tibetan Mountains (Shambhala?). The occultists affirm that these "men" possess great powers and are able to control invisible forces in the spiritual realm. They apparently can prolong their lives for centuries and, in so doing, are forever guiding humanity's destiny by influencing key people on earth. The Great White Brotherhood is often associated with the "Great White Lodge," an invisible brotherhood which exists in the ethereal realm that surrounds the earth. Are the Ascended Masters of the Great White Brotherhood (or Great White Lodge) both physical and spirit beings?

They're All in Cahoots

Accompanying Count Saint Germain and Master *Jesus* in this Great White Brotherhood council are Sanat Kumara, Bodhisattva Maitreya, Master Koot Hoomi (or Kuthumi), Master Djual Khool (or Djwhal Khul), Manu Vaivasvata, Master Morya, Master Jupiter, Maha Chohan, the Venetion Master, Master Serapis, Master Hilarion, and Master Prince Rakoczi.

Master Prince Rakoczi and Count Saint Germain are, in all likelihood, the same person. In 1774 Count Saint Germain appeared in Nuremberg, Germany, claiming to be Prince Rakoczy, one of three brothers from Transylvania; although at that time, all three brothers were dead. It has been reported that Prince Rakoczi (as a spirit being or a physical being) speaks many languages. Similarly, during Count Saint Germain's stay in Europe, he often spoke fluent French, German, English, Dutch, and Russian and claimed to know Chinese, Hindu, and Persian as well.

It is interesting to note that Master *Jesus,* Master Koot Hoomi, Master Djwhal Khul, Master Morya, Master Hilarion, and Master Prince Rakoczi were all originally contacted by Madame Blavatsky, who even maintained that some of her communications with these "Masters" were face to face.

Additionally, other communications from these "Masters" occurred paranormally when specific notes and letters, signed with the Master's initials mysteriously materialized in unexpected places. Other letters from the Masters resembled channeled messages via automatic writing. It appears that Blavatsky was, in fact, a medium through which contact with the Masters took place.

This collection of messages is known as the Mahatma Letters, and some of the original documents are on display at the British Library in London. It would appear that Madame Blavatsky was the first primary contact (or channel?) of the Ascended Masters of the Great White Brotherhood.

These Ascended Masters of the Great White Brotherhood are recognized by George King's Aetherius Society as "extraterrestrials" and are given the title "Cosmic Masters." It is interesting to note that in 1954, while King was meditating in his home in London, he was visited by a mysterious Indian yoga master. This "master" informed King that "Cosmic Intelligences" had selected him to be their primary channel.

Since the 1950s, contactee Gabriel Green, who has witnessed over one hundred sightings of flying saucers, claims to be in contact (both physically and telepathically) with the "Space Masters" of the Great White Brotherhood. These outer space beings instructed him to organize the Amalgamated Flying Saucer Clubs of America (AFSCA), which he did in 1959. AFSCA quickly became popular, boasting over five thousand members in twenty-four countries.

In 1984 Green channeled a specific message from Ashtar regarding the imminent return of the Aquarian Age Christ. Ashtar informed Green that the second coming of "the Christ" will occur when a spaceship makes its first public landing. "The Christ" will, of course, be on board.

A Prime Cut: Church Universal and Triumphant

The impact of the Great White Brotherhood seems to have repercussions in our society. After the death of Guy Ballard in 1939, channeled communications within the "I Am" Movement diminished. So in the 1950s, another team of messengers arose that replaced the Ballards, namely Mark L. Prophet (1918-1973) and his wife, Elizabeth Clare Wulf Prophet (born 8 April 1940 in New Jersey).

Influenced by the theosophical teachings of the "I Am" Religious Activity, Mark Prophet organized a church called the Summit Lighthouse in 1958 in Washington, D.C. For several years he had been channeling messages from the Ascended Masters of the Great White Brotherhood. In 1961 he met Elizabeth, and she too became a messenger of the brotherhood. In 1962, as a direct result of channeled communications with ascended master Saint Germain, they established the Keepers of the Flame Fraternity. In 1966 they relocated to Colorado Springs, Colorado.

One year after Mark's death in 1974, Summit Lighthouse became incorporated by Elizabeth Clare Prophet as the Church Universal and Triumphant (CUT). She has since taken full responsibility as the sole appointed messenger of the Ascended Masters of the Great White Brotherhood. In 1976 the church's headquarters moved to Pasadena, California. Ten years later they finally settled in Montana near the Teton Mountain range which borders Yellowstone National Park.

Interestingly enough, Elizabeth Clare Prophet (also known as Guru Ma) now broadcasts her worship services nationally on cable television. Her teachings are based upon her channeled transmissions from the "Lords of the Flame," including: Count Saint Germain, *Jesus,* Koot Hoomi, El Morya, and many other "ascended masters." Prophet also claims that the Blessed Virgin Mary, known in the spirit world as "Lady Nada," frequently visits her. The church claims membership in the tens of thousands.

Mark of the Age

It just so happens that Lady Nada is also a channeled entity of Nada-Yolanda (Pauline Sharpe), the primary channeler for the Florida-based organization Mark-Age, Inc. Other channeled entities include Sananda, Djwhal Khul, El Morya, and even Gloria Lee. Since 1960, Mark-Age has been channeling messages from this spiritual hierarchy believed to be orbiting the earth in spaceships. Members of Mark-Age await the second coming of the Aquarian-Age Christ, which is supposed to take place around the year 2000.

We, the Arcturians

In the spring of 1985, Norma J. Milanovich began channeling messages via automatic writing on her personal computer from a group of extraterrestrial beings known as the "Celestials." These "Celestials," who also claim to be orbiting the earth in spaceships, come from the bright star Arcturus, which is located in the constellation Bootes. These Arcturians represent heaven's "Celestial Command" of the "Galactic Command." Their mission is to help fulfill the designated plan of Sananda (also known as *Jesus the Christ*), Ashtar, Kuthumi (also known as "The World Teacher"), and other so-called Ascended Masters of the Universe (i.e., the Great White Brotherhood).

Several Arcturians transmitting messages through Milanovich are Juluionno (commander of the Starship Athena), Herdonitic (an Elder of the Starship Athena), Ascheana (a female crew member of the Starship Athena), and Arturo, a guide from the Starship Athena. In fact, Ashtar Command members Monka and Soltec also channel messages through Milanovich. It should be noted here that Athena is coincidentally recognized by the Ashtar Command as a female *commander* of the Starship of Sananda. Does Athena, in fact, have a duel designation? Or, is this simply an undetected error?

Not long after these outer space transmissions began in Milanovich's life, she received assistance and support from two friends, Betty Rice and Cynthia Ploski. These three (perhaps another *female occult trinity*) regularly participated in weekly channeling sessions with the "Celestials." In 1990, after nine months of telepathic communications, their collaborative effort was recorded in their book *We, the Arcturians*.

In recent years it seems that Milanovich has become the primary channeler for Kuthumi. These channeled messages contain revelations pertaining to cataclysmic changes on earth that will take place between 1991 and 2011. Kuthumi also claims that earth will eventually transform into a star. At that time only individuals with a higher consciousness will enter into a fifth dimension, that is, another reality that parallels our physical world. This other reality may only be perceived by those with a higher consciousness.

If You Build It They Will Come

Kuthumi's activities seem endless. He has also initiated the building of an earth energy system, known as the "Templar" project in Crestone, Colorado (a possible power spot). The goal of this project is to help the earth realign itself with the universe as it moves through the solar system during this transitional period. In 1991 Milanovich founded the Trinity Foundation in Albuquerque, New Mexico, to assist in this project. The Templar will be a huge, pink, granite-faced pyramid with an obsidian (a black, hard volcanic glass) capstone. This structure will be surrounded by a hexagonal wall. The Templar's unique design will enable it to receive and store divine energies directed toward the earth from the "Most High."

It is interesting to note that during the summer of 1967, anomalous lights were reported approximately twenty miles south of Crestone in the San Luis valley area. On 8 September 1967, a mutilated horse was discovered in this area (an event which was well publicized). Concomitant with this event were reports of UFO sightings. Shortly thereafter, in mid-September, a Denver man witnessed three slow moving UFOs below the tops of the Sangre De Cristo Mountain range, which is a few miles southeast of Crestone. The area not only turned into a media circus, but also became the focus of rigorous investigations. People flocked to the area for many years hoping to see a UFO or encounter some kind of paranormal phenomena.

Another proposed structure to be built is the "Extraterrestrial Embassy." On 13 December 1973 French race car driver and journalist Claude Vorilhon (born 1946), also known as "Rael," claims to have had an encounter with extraterrestrial beings near a volcanic mountain range in France. These beings, known as the "Elohim," commissioned Rael to construct this embassy in Jerusalem by 2025. When the structure is completed, the Elohim will arrive in spaceships and meet with our scientists and political leaders to share their wisdom and technology. To the amazement of all, accompanying the Elohim will be every prophet from every religion including Jesus, Moses, Buddha, and Mohammed (who apparently were their messengers)!

The Raelian Movement rapidly blossomed into an international organization and currently boasts over forty thousand members worldwide. The Movement has locations in the United States, Canada, France, Switzerland, and Japan. Rael's books are translated into twenty-five languages.

On a similar note, in the 1950s George Van Tassel, who founded the now defunct Ministry of Universal Wisdom, channeled messages from Solganda instructing him to build a device known as the "Integratron." This machine, a four-story high domed structure, was supposed to rejuvenate the elderly and stop the aging process of our youth. According to Van Tassel, during the course of construction, the Integratron displayed unusual images apparently coming from another time frame. Even though he spent nearly 200,000 dollars, it was never completed, and Van Tassel died. Was this Integratron, in fact, a kind of time machine?

Invasion of the Body Snatchers

Sedona, Arizona, known for its scenic red rock mountains and canyons, is another popular gathering place for psychics, channelers, and New Age disciples. From 1986 to 1993, it was the home of the UFO movement known as the "Extraterrestrial Earth Mission."

The Mission's leaders, Savizar and Silarra, are two channelers who claim to be extraterrestrials inhabiting human bodies. In fact, there have been numerous extraterrestrials occupying and possessing these same humans for years. For example, in 1986, Savizar was a different entity known as Avinash, and Silarra was called Arthea. In the summer of 1987 (during the Harmonic Convergence), Avinash became Aktivar, and Arthea became Akria. In March

1988, Aktivar and Akria were replaced by Alarius and Polaria, respectively. Soon afterwards the couple became known as Savizar and Silarra. In 1990 Savizar was replaced by a being called ZaviRah, and Silarra changed to Ziva'rah. Then in 1993, Drakar and Zrendar replaced ZaviRah and Ziva'rah and moved the Mission to Hawaii. Since that time, their assignment, known as the "Christ Star Project," has been to facilitate the evolutionary process of the New Age Movement by co-creating a "new civilization" (i.e., "Heaven") on earth.

Are these extraterrestrial "walk-ins," in fact, modern day manifestations of the age-old "familiar spirits" recorded in the Old Testament of the Bible? This invites serious consideration (cf., Deut. 18:9-14; 1 Sam. 28:3-20; Isa. 8:19-20 KJV).

One afternoon in 1987, an Arizona UFO metaphysical group of about fifty-five people gathered in Sedona and witnessed a remarkable and astonishingly unusual formation of clouds in the sky clearly spelling out the word YAHWEH. After the clouds quickly dissipated, three inexplicable red glowing lights appeared over a nearby hill. Each light went out consecutively as nightfall approached.

Over the years, Sedona has played host to a wide variety of paranormal phenomena, including UFO sightings, strange cavorting lights, fairy confrontations, visions of "spirits" including the Blessed Virgin Mary, and other unusual manifestations. The Yavapai Indians, incidentally, consider Sedona to be a sacred area, and their myths reveal that an assortment of "deities" live in the rocks.

Another extraterrestrial walk-in is Shaari, a female entity from the "Star Command." In 1989 she inhabited the body of a human trance medium who vacated after an automobile accident. Shortly thereafter she organized the Trilite Seminars. Shaari continues to follow in the footsteps of her predecessors, channeling messages from Abraham, a male entity claiming to be a member of the "Light Brotherhood" and the "Intergalactic Command," and a female entity known as Malaya.

Occult Trinity Revisited

The Trilite Seminars, held regularly throughout the United States and Canada, consist of workshops, private individual sessions, and triennial retreats. Some of these retreats are held at locations considered to be "power spots." Curiously enough, the threesome that spearhead the Trilite Seminars are none other than Shaari, Abraham, and Malaya (Melton 1996a). Is this, in fact, another *occult trinity* at work?

In summary, it has become more and more apparent that the UFO phenomenon, the Occult, and the New Age Movement have consciously or unconsciously banded together as a socio-religious force for the express purpose of creating and fostering a New World Order. Are the UFO phenomenon, the Occult, and the New Age Movement the ultimate *occult trinity?*

Chapter 5

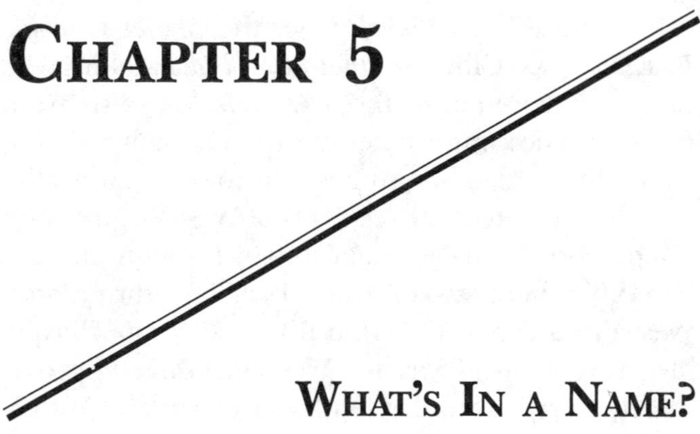

What's In a Name?

Woodrow W. Derenberger

One wet Wednesday evening on 2 November 1966 near Mineral Wells, West Virginia, Woodrow W. Derenberger (b. 1916) had a face to face encounter with a "man" claiming to be from outer space. This spaceman, who came out of a spaceship, telepathically communicated to "Woody" that his name was *Cold.* Two days later, on November 4 near Parkersburg, West Virginia, Derenberger had another telepathic contact with Cold. During this second contact, Woody was informed that Cold resided on the planet *Lanulos* (a planet almost identical to earth), located near the galaxy of Ganymede (one of Jupiter's moons). He had a wife named *Kimi* and a new born daughter, *Kimilis.* Before telepathic contact was broken, however, Cold revealed that his first name was *Indrid.*

Thereafter, many contacts (both telepathically and physically) took place between Woody Derenberger and *Indrid Cold.* Through Cold, Derenberger met other supposed residents of Lanulos, including: *Karl Ardo,* second in command of the spaceship; *Clinnel,* from the planet *Cerabus; Bueldine Vaus,* Clinnel's wife; *Jitro Cletaw* and his wife *Elvane,* from Venus; and *Demo Hassan,* also from Cerabus. These same outer space beings, it is claimed, communicated (either physically or telepathically) with at least ten other residents of West Virginia and Ohio. Also, from November 1966 through December 1967, there was a major UFO "flap" throughout West Virginia and the Ohio River valley, specifically targeting Point Pleasant, West Virginia (approximately thirty-five miles southwest of Mineral Wells).

The Germans Are Coming

During the decades of the 1930s and the 1940s, German scientists Hermann Oberth (1894—1989), Wernher von Braun (1912—1977), and *Walter Doernberger* conducted numerous experiments involving rocket flight. They later developed the V-1 and V-2 rockets that wreaked havoc over European skies during World War II. Concurrent with these developments was the manufacture of TNT in Point Pleasant, West Virginia. These high explosives were stored in various underground tunnels outside the city.

Interestingly enough, in 1945, Wernher von Braun and many other German rocket scientists were recruited by the United States Army to help develop its guided missile program. Later, von Braun became director of the National Aeronautics and Space Administration (NASA).

Semantics or Some Antics Again

A few months after Derenberger's alleged contacts with beings from other planets, he met two other contactees while lecturing in Westford, Massachusetts. One claimed to be in telepathic communication with *Umar* of Jupiter, while the other communicated telepathically with *Orthon* of Venus.

George Adamski, if you recall, was the first person to make contact with Orthon of Venus (noted in chapter one). He purportedly met two other "men" from outer space—*Firkon,* who supposedly resided on Mars, and *Ramu* (Umar spelled backwards), who claimed residence on Saturn. Of utmost importance here is the fact that Orthon, Firkon, and Ramu were not the real names of these spacemen. In the first chapter of his book *Inside the Space Ships* (1955), Adamski clearly states that the real names of these spacemen were never given to him and that he specifically named them Orthon, Firkon, and Ramu for a particular reason. What was his reason?

Throughout this book, we have uncovered many suspiciously odd and unusual names of so-called extraterrestrials or otherworldly beings. Are there any underlying meanings attached to these names?

The day after Adamski's death, on 24 April 1965, Arthur Bryant of England had a conversation with a spaceman identifying himself as *Yamski.* Just five months earlier in December 1964, again in England, Arthur Shuttlewood was visited at his home by *Caellsan, Selorik,* and *Traellison,* three spacemen from the planet *Aenstria.*

Between these incidents, on 30 January 1965 near Monterey, California, Sidney Padrick was invited aboard a landed spacecraft by a spaceman identifying himself as *Zeeno* (or *Xeno*). A little over seven years earlier, on 5 November 1957 Reinhold Schmidt was invited aboard a blimp-shaped object in Kearney, Nebraska, by its captain, *Mr. X,* who informed Schmidt that he and his outer space companions were from Saturn.

Howard Menger (born 1922), a popular contactee

of the 1950s, lived on a farm near High Bridge, New Jersey. During 1956 and 1957, he claimed numerous contacts with Venusians, Martians, and Saturnians (like that of Adamski). These space people informed him that he was originally a spiritual teacher named *Sol da Naro* on Saturn. Strangely, he divorced his wife so he could marry *Marla* (Constance Weber), an alleged spacewoman from the planet Venus. Marla, in her book *My Saturnian Lover* (1958), recognized Menger by his other space name, *Alyn.*

Numerous other suspiciously odd or apparently significant names of supposed extraterrestrials (or unearthly beings) have surfaced throughout the last fifty years. Dates and/or names and/or locations associated with these names are as follows:

1. Quazgaa, Joohoop, Andantio (25 January 1967 Betty Andreasson Luca [Christian abductee], South Ashburnham, Massachusetts)
2. Aramda (1958, Peru)
3. Orlon (1967, U.S.)
4. Ishtar ([i.e., the ancient Babylonian goddess of love, fertility, and war], 26 December 1985 Whitley Strieber [born 1945; abductee], upstate New York)
5. Sfath, Asket, Semjase (Billy Meier [contactee], Switzerland)
6. Kalna, Ilmuth (1950s, George Adamski)
7. Krlll (1954, President Eisenhower)
8. Baloran, Ray-mere, Sut-ko (Aleuti Francesca [channeler], Solar Light Retreat, White City, Oregon)
9. Adonai, Aljanon, Alphon, Amorania, Andolo, Andromeda Rex, Anton, Arcturus, Argus, Armeda, Arunada, Avalon, Cassion, Cetti,

Crystal Love, James, Kadar Monka, Klala, Kren Lor, El Morya, ESU (Jesus the Christ), Excelsior, Hatonn, Hermes, Hilarion, Joshua, Jycondria, Lytton, Maitreya, Matton, Melchior, (Lord) Michael, Munton, Nada, Nathant, Oriel, Paul (the Venetian), Philip, Rowena, Sanat Kumara, Tarvis, Teska, Thedra, Tonanias, Vegan (Ashtar's son), Venus, Voltra, Xylatra, Xyletron, Zoser (1980s, 1990s; channeled through Tuella and others involved with the Ashtar Command)

10. Ashtar Sheran (1957, Germany)
11. (Mr.) Apol, Lia (1967, Point Pleasant, West Virginia)
12. Akon, Ayling (i.e., Akon's son) (1956, Elizabeth Klarer [contactee], Johannesburg, South Africa)
13. Basher, Anima (1983, Darryl Anka [channeler], Interplanetary Connections, California)
14. Nacoma (1958, United States)
15. Linn-Erri (July 1961, Massachusetts)
16. Ausso One (25 October 1974 Carl Higdon, Wyoming)
17. Aphloes (May 1967, Long Island, New York)
18. Kronin (26 July 1967 California)
19. Zandark (September 1973, Georgia)
20. Karnu (1960s)

Similarly, various channelers also adopt unusual names including:

1. Alta (Ernest Norman)
2. Ellyssa (Tuella's daughter)
3. Camhael, Obid, Tuieta (Ashtar Command)

Other planets with interesting names include:

1. Blaau, Cerus, Erra (Semjase), Fowser, Korendor, Maldek, Maser, Metharia, Meton, Schare (Van Tassel), and Zomdic.

Other significant terms include:

1. Nova Terra (spaceship earth, Ashtar Command)
2. Titans (a race of giants that once lived on earth)
3. Tefra (ethereal plane, Ashtar Command)
4. Satonian (a negative race of beings, Ashtar Command)
5. Merkabah (New Jerusalem City energy device, Ashtar Command)
6. DAL (universe, Billy Meier)
7. Shan (earth, Ashtar Command)
8. Terra (earth, Ashtar Command)
9. ShanChea (earth satellite, Ashtar Command)
10. Adonai Vassu (a greeting used in communications from Zandark)
11. Kazik (a term used by Al Bender to contact various outer space entities; sometimes recognized as the name of a planet)

Within the UFO phenomenon, I have observed numerous coincidental appearances of the first names "George" and "Betty." These comprise a body of contactees, abductees, and UFO witnesses. Some examples are:

1. *George* Adamski
2. *George* and *Betty* Williamson
3. Al and *Betty* Bailey
4. *Betty* Bowen (a witness to Williamson's outer space contacts)
5. *George* Van Tassel
6. *Betty* Bender (Al Bender's wife)

7. *George* King
8. *Betty* Hill (abductee; White Mountains, New Hampshire; 19-20 September 1961)
9. *George* O'Barski (UFO incident involving occupants; North Hudson Park, New Jersey; 12 January 1975)
10. *Betty* Cash (a cancer victim as a direct result of radiation poisoning after witnessing a UFO near Huffman, Texas; 29 December 1980)
11. *Betty* Ann Behl (Air Force weather observer who witnessed the July 1952 UFO sightings over Washington, D.C.)
12. *Betty* Mitchell (contactee of the 1950s)
13. *Betty* Rice
14. *Betty* Andreasson Luca

The Betty Book

On 17 March 1919 the name Betty became the focus of attention when Stuart Edward White (1873-1946) and a group of friends decided to dabble with a ouija board. To their amazement, after only a few attempts at contacting the spirit world, the pointer (a whiskey glass) began to move and repeatedly spell out the name "Betty." *Betty* White (Stuart's wife), who was not participating with the group at the time, disapproved of the group's actions. However, after witnessing the phenomenon, she reluctantly placed her fingertips on the glass. At that precise moment, the pointer started going crazy, making circles and spelling out the phrase "get a pencil." This spawned a series of contacts via automatic writing and channeling with unseen entities through Betty White for nearly twenty years. As a direct result of these channeled communications, *The Betty Book*, which was written and published by her husband in 1937, revealed startling "New Age" concepts.

A Secret Code Revealed

Occasionally a breakthrough occurs in the research of UFOs. One such milestone is Allen H. Greenfield's book *Secret Cipher of the UFOnauts* (1994). It is an achievement that has earned the utmost respect of this author. Greenfield's painstaking effort yielded a secret code known as "Cypher 6" that has been used by magicians and occultists throughout the world. The Cypher 6 code converts each letter of the alphabet into a number. Coincidentally, the Cypher 6 code is based on the number "11," which is considered by occultists to be the great sacred number of *magick.* By counting down eleven letters of the alphabet after the letter "A" (A=1), the Cypher 6 code emerges by consecutively numbering each letter in sequence (L=2, W=3, H=4, and so on) until all letters of the alphabet are assigned a numerical value. Additionally, I have discovered the significance of the numbers nineteen and seven and have augmented the code by including a plus nineteen or a minus seven in the sequence.

The Cipher 6 Code

(with the +19 and -7 additions)

A = 1	(2) N = 14 (-7)
(1) B = 20 (+19)	(3) O = 7 (-7)
(2) C = 13 (-7)	(4) P = 26 (+19)
(3) D = 6 (-7)	(5) Q = 19 (-7)
(4) E = 25 (+19)	(6) R = 12 (-7)
(5) F = 18 (-7)	(7) S = 5 (-7)
(6) G = 11 (-7)	(8) T = 24 (+19)
(7) H = 4 (-7)	(9) U = 17 (-7)
(8) I = 23 (+19)	(10) V = 10 (-7)
(9) J = 16 (-7)	(11) W = 3 (-7)
(10) K = 9 (-7)	(1) X = 22 (+19)

(11) L = 2 (-7) (2) Y = 15 (-7)
(1) M = 21 (+19) (3) Z = 8 (-7)

In his book, Greenfield applies the Cypher 6 code to the various odd names involved with the UFO phenomenon. After converting each name into a number, he discovered that certain names have equivalent numerical values. These numerical values have added a relational dimension to the names that would not normally be uncovered.

The following tables (consisting of numbers one through nine) apply the Cypher 6 code to the suspiciously odd and apparently significant names revealed thus far in this book.

The total numerical value of each name is determined by adding the number value of each letter together. For example:

A + S + H + T + A + R
1 + 5 + 4 + 24 + 1 + 12 = 47
47 = 4 + 7 = 11
11 = 1 + 1 = 2
ASHTAR = 47 = 11 = 2

In numerology, 2 is the digital root of 47 and therefore the number of the name Ashtar. Ashtar is subsequently listed under Table 2 (or number 2). Remember that 2 is also derived from 11, the sacred magical number of occultists.

Table 1 (Number 1)

SAINT GERMAIN = 136 = 10 = 1
AETHERIUS = 136 = 10 = 1
RAKOCZI = 73 = 10 = 1
KORTON = 73 = 10 = 1
ARTURO = 73 = 10 = 1
SATURN = 73 = 10 = 1

DJWHAL KHUL = 64 = 10 = 1
ASCHEANNA = 64 = 10 = 1
HATONN = 64 = 10 = 1
ASKET = 64 = 10 = 1
TESKA = 64 = 10 = 1
MASER = 64 = 10 = 1
MALDEK = 64 = 10 = 1
LADY NADA = 46 = 10 =1
SHAARI = 46 = 10 = 1
AKRIA = 46 = 10 = 1
ARGUS = 46 = 10 = 1
PAUL = 46 = 10 = 1
J.W. = 19 = 10 = 1
RO = 19 = 10 = 1
KOOT HOOMI = 109 = 10 = 1
CETTI = 109 = 10 = 1
NATHANT = 82 = 10 = 1
ANTARES = 82 = 10 = 1
ELOHIM = 82 = 10 = 1
MR. X = 55 = 10 = 1
SOL DA NARO = 55 = 10 = 1
ALJANON = 55 = 10 = 1
ELLYSSA = 55 = 10 = 1
ANDOLO = 37 = 10 = 1
MARLA = 37 = 10 = 1
MANU VAIVASVATA = 118 = 10 = 1
GANYMEDE = 118 = 10 = 1
ILMUTH = 91 = 10 = 1
GEORGE = 91 = 10 = 1
MATTON = 91 = 10 = 1
TITANS = 91 = 10 = 1
METON = 91 = 10 = 1
LATA = 28 = 10 = 1
ALTA = 28 = 10 = 1
COLD = 28 = 10 = 1

Table 2 (Number 2 or 11)

ASHTAR = 47 = 11 = 2
SOLGANDA = 47 = 11 = 2
CLOTA = 47 = 11 = 2
ESU = 47 = 11 = 2
FIRKON = 83 = 11 = 2
SELORIK = 83 = 11 = 2
EL MORYA = 83 = 11 = 2
MORYA = 56 = 11 = 2
SILARRA = 56 = 11 = 2
VOLTRA = 56 = 11 = 2
OBID = 56 = 11 = 2
MASSAI = 56 = 11 = 2
PONNAR = 74 = 11 = 2
SINGBA = 74 = 11 = 2
JOOHOOP = 74 = 11 = 2
ELEX = 74 = 11 = 2
YAMSKI = 74 = 11 = 2
TERRA = 74 = 11 = 2
AFFA = 38 = 11 = 2
UM = 38 = 11 = 2
VASSU = 38 = 11 = 2
KADAR = 29 = 11 = 2
ADAM = 29 = 11 = 2
AURA RHANES = 92 = 11 = 2
HERMES = 92 = 11 = 2
KORENDOR = 92 = 11 = 2
LOCKTOPAR = 101 = 2
LUCIFER = 110 = 2
GREAT CENTRAL SUN = 200 = 2
ETHERIAN = 128 = 11 = 2

Table 3 (Number 3)

EARTH = 66 = 12 = 3
ADAMSKI = 66 = 12 = 3

ARMEDA = 66 = 12 = 3
AYLING = 66 = 12 = 3
DEVIL = 66 = 12 = 3
CLATU = 57 = 12 = 3
ZOSER = 57 = 12 = 3
BALORAN = 57 = 12 = 3
CLINNEL = 93 = 12 = 3
MERKABAH = 93 = 12 = 3
AURA RAINES = 111 = 3
RAY- MERE = 111 = 3
TEMPLAR = 111 = 3
RIC = 48 = 12 = 3
LANULOS = 48 = 12 = 3
BAQRAUN = 84 = 12 = 3
LATAMARX = 84 = 12 = 3
INDRID = 84 = 12 = 3
HULDA = 30 = 3
NADA = 30 = 3
OBLOW = 39 = 12 = 3
MARS = 39 = 12 = 3
OARA = 21 = 3
TARVIS = 57 = 12 = 3

Table 4 (Number 4)

AVINASH = 58 = 13 = 4
QUAZGAA = 58 = 13 = 4
TOUKA = 58 = 13 = 4
ARTHEA = 67 = 13 = 4
COSMON = 67 = 13 = 4
CAMHAEL = 67 = 13 = 4
SHANCHEA = 67 = 13 = 4
MARK III = 112 = 4
INDRID COLD = 112 = 4
SOLTEC = 76 = 13 = 4
KIMI = 76 = 13 = 4
PLUTO = 76 = 13 = 4

RAEL = 40 = 4

(The Elohim informed Rael that his mission is the last of 40 prophets.)

NORO = 40 = 4

MARY = 49 = 13 = 4

(Visions of the Blessed Virgin Mary frequently occur consecutively on the 13th of each month.)

GUARDIAN = 85 = 13 = 4

SISTER THEDRA = 166 = 13 = 4

AKON = 31 = 4

XYLETRON = 121 = 4

Table 5 (Number 5)

ORTHON = 68 = 14 = 5
JESUS = 68 = 14 = 5
LOMEC = 68 = 14 = 5
NADA-YOLANDA = 68 = 14 = 5
XENO = 68 = 14 = 5
CASSION = 68 = 14 = 5
JAMES = 68 = 14 = 5
MAITREYA = 122 = 5
VALIANT THOR = 122 = 5
SHAMBHALA = 59 = 14 = 5
ZAVIRAH = 59 = 14 = 5
ZIVARAH = 59 = 14 = 5
HILARION = 86 = 14 = 5
LYTTON = 86 = 14 = 5
MALAYA = 41 = 5
DRAKAR = 41 = 5
BLAAU = 41 = 5
JOSHUA = 50 = 5
KAZIK = 50 = 5
LEEKTOW = 95 = 14 = 5
INTEGRATRON = 167 = 14 = 5
ALYN = 32 = 5

WAN (-4) = 14 = 5
XYLATRA = 77 = 14 = 5
PHILIP = 104 = 5
JESUS CHRIST = 149 = 14 = 5

Table 6 (Number 6)

SANANDA = 42 = 6
ORLON = 42 = 6
ARAMDA = 42 = 6
SAVIZAR = 60 = 6
KUMAR = 60 = 6
REGGA = 60 = 6
ANTON = 60 = 6
ANIMA = 60 = 6
ABRAHAM = 60 = 6
SCHARE = 60 = 6
ROMILAR = 78 = 15 = 6
ZRENDAR = 78 = 15 = 6
ZOMDIC = 78 = 15 = 6
ATHENA = 69 = 15 = 6
SOLAR STAR = 69 = 15 = 6
ISHTAR = 69 = 15 = 6
ORIEL = 69 = 15 = 6
NOSTRO = 69 = 15 = 6
RAMU = 51 = 6
UMAR = 51 = 6
ACTAR = 51 = 6
ZANDARK = 51 = 6
ADU = 24 = 6
SHAN = 24 = 6
ZO = 15 = 6
KLALA = 15 = 6
ANKAR (-22) = 15 = 6
SUTTKU = 96 = 15 = 6
LACU = 33 = 6

TUIETA = 114 = 6
AENSTRIA = 105 = 6
THE ETHERIANS = 186 = 15 = 6

Table 7 (Number 7)

MONKA = 52 = 7
ADONAI = 52 = 7
YAHWEH = 52 = 7
ARUNADA = 52 = 7
SFATH = 52 = 7
SANAT KUMARA = 106 = 7
MOHAMMED = 106 = 7
NOVA TERRA = 106 = 7
KUTHUMI = 115 = 7
TRAELLISON = 115 = 7
MERCURY = 115 = 7
MAHA CHOHAN = 70 = 7
APHLOES = 70 = 7
FOWSER = 70 = 7
SERAPIS = 97 = 16 = 7
MUNTON = 97 = 16 = 7
ALARIUS = 61 = 7
VEGAN = 61 = 7
SEDAT = 61 = 7
SHAMBALLAH = 61 = 7
URIEL = 79 = 16 = 7
KERRULL = 79 = 16 = 7
ZEENO = 79 = 16 = 7
KRONIN = 79 = 16 = 7
NOMA = 43 = 7
BASHAR = 43 = 7
ZRS = 25 = 7
HERDONITIC = 151 = 7
VENETION = 142 = 7
ETHERIANS = 133 = 7

Table 8 (Number 8)

ALOMAR = 44 = 8
MOLCA = 44 = 8
ZEHAAS = 44 = 8
DJUAL KHOOL = 71 = 8
TUELLA = 71 = 8
VENUS = 71 = 8
AKTIVAR = 80 = 8
AMORANIA = 80 = 8
TEFRA = 80 = 8
ELCAR = 53 = 8
KARNU = 53 = 8
SUT-KO = 62 = 8
ROWENA = 62 = 8
LIA = 26 = 8
ARDO = 26 = 8
DEMO HASSAN = 89 = 17 = 8
TONANIAS = 89 = 17 = 8
MICHAEL = 89 = 17 = 8
SATONIAN = 89 = 17 = 8
JYCONDRIA = 107 = 8
MELCHIOR = 107 = 8
JUPITER = 143 = 8
I AM THAT I AM = 143 = 8
SEMJASE = 98 = 17 = 8
CRYSTAL LOVE = 188 = 17 = 8
ANDROMEDA REX = 152 = 8
EXCELSIOR = 134 = 8
AVALON = 35 = 8

Table 9 (Number 9)

POLARIA = 72 = 9
PORTLA = 72 = 9
THEDRA = 72 = 9
CLARION = 72 = 9

CERUS = 72 = 9
KADAR MONKA = 81 = 9
KREN LOR = 81 = 9
CHRIST = 81 = 9
AUSSO ONE = 81 = 9
APOL = 36 = 9
GARR = 36 = 9
LUU = 36 = 9
ZAGO = 27 = 9
KALNA = 27 = 9
KRLLL = 27 = 9
ASHTAR SHERAN = 108 = 9
LUTBUNN = 108 = 9
BETTY = 108 = 9
ALPHON = 54 = 9
BUDDHA = 54 = 9
CAELLSAN = 63 = 9
MOSES = 63 = 9
ORION = 63 = 9
JULUIONNO = 117 = 9
LORD MICHAEL = 117 = 9
ANDANTIO = 90 = 9
ADONAI VASSU = 90 = 9
GUARDIANS = 90 = 9
A-LAN = 18 = 9
666 = 18 = 9
I AM = 45 = 9
SATAN = 45 = 9
DAL = 9

In the preceding nine tables, the numerical value of each name has been catalogued. It has become clear that certain names have the same *numerical* value. When the first numerical value (i.e., the larger number) of two or more names is identical, it may, in fact, mean that we are dealing with the same entity or that the words or names are somehow associated with the entity. Also, it is possible that a secret, unknown meaning lies behind the transmitted messages given to human contacts by these entities. If this is the case, to whom are these coded messages directed and for what purpose?

Interestingly enough, some ancient cultures believed that the *real* names of their various gods, angels, and demons were carefully concealed and literally kept secret. It was considered taboo to know a god's real name. Why?

Following a similar cultural pattern, one particular occurrence in the Bible illuminates us concerning an undisclosed angelic name:

> And Manoah said unto the angel of the Lord, "What is thy name, that when thy sayings come to pass we may do thee honor?" And the angel of the Lord said unto him, "Why askest thou thus after my name, seeing it is secret?" (Judges 13:17-18)

Hidden codes even appear in *We, the Arcturians* by Milanovich, Rice, and Ploski. In the preface of their book, they inform the reader outright that certain sections of their book may contain a particular code to help one survive during the "New Age."

Similarly, in the book *Ashtar*, compiled by Tuella, Ashtar informs Tuella that certain spiritual beings of the Ashtar Command use coded names, especially names that begin with the letter "A," "T," or "K." Each letter supposedly signifies a different degree of the Ashtar Command's "mission" involving planet Earth.

Devices or tactics such as these may, in fact, be what the Apostle Paul was alluding to in his New Testament letter when he instructed the Corinthian Christians:

> . . . lest Satan should get an advantage of us: for we are not ignorant of his devices. (II Cor. 2:11)

Earlier in this chapter, we briefly mentioned an outer space entity named *Apol* (or Mr. Apol). Apol communicated (both physically and telepathically) with certain individuals in Point Pleasant, West Virginia, during the intense UFO activity period between 1966 and 1967.

Is it possible that the name Apol is actually an etymological derivation of the name *Apol*lyon (or Satan) as revealed by the Apostle John in the Bible's prophetic book of Revelation?

> And they had a king over them, which is the angel of the bottomless pit, whose name in the Hebrew tongue is Abaddon, but in the Greek tongue hath his name Apollyon. (Rev. 9:11)

(As noted in Table 9, the numerical values, or digital root, of the names Apol and Satan are equivalent.)

Transformation

Like Mr. Apol, Indrid Cold, Orthon, and many others, it would appear that these twentieth century "extraterrestrials" are able to transform themselves into human-like beings. The Apostle Paul further illuminates us regarding Satanic transformation. In another of his letters, he states:

> For such are false apostles, deceitful workers, transforming themselves into the apostles of Christ. And no marvel; for Satan himself is transformed into an angel of light. Therefore it is no great thing if his ministers also be transformed as the ministers of righteousness; whose end shall be according to their works. (II Cor. 11:13-15)

Possession

Apparently these so-called extraterrestrials also possess the power to take over (or occupy) the bodies of certain individuals. The New Testament of the Bible recounts numerous circumstances regarding the possession of human beings by *evil* spirits or *"devils"* (i.e., *demons*):

> And when he was come to the other side into the country of the Gergesenes, there met him two possessed with devils [demons], coming out of the tombs, exceeding fierce, so that no man might pass by that way. (Matt. 8:28)

Other biblical examples include: Matthew 9:32; 15:22; 17:14-18; Mark 1:23-28; Luke 8:2-3; and Acts 5:16; 16:16-18; 19:11-20.

Are these "masked" outer space entities, in fact, an organized legion of *demonic* beings participating in the ingenious, yet sinister, "alien" plan devised by their "Commander in Chief," *Satan?* If so, does this "plan" require the communication of coded messages to certain important and powerful political and religious leaders for undisclosed reasons? Is it possible that these political and religious leaders, either knowingly or unknowingly, are actually pawns of Satan to ultimately deceive the entire population?

Remember, Satan battled for the *soul* of Simon Peter:

> And the Lord said, Simon, Simon, behold, Satan hath desired to have you, that he may sift you as wheat. (Luke 22:31)

Is this battle continuing today, jeopardizing millions of human *souls?* Are Satan and his emissaries, in fact, posing as extraterrestrials? As we sift through the intricate maze so characteristic of the UFO phenomenon, one question continues to haunt us. Will we, in the end, find ourselves standing face to face staring directly into the penetrating eyes of the "Arch Deceiver," Satan?

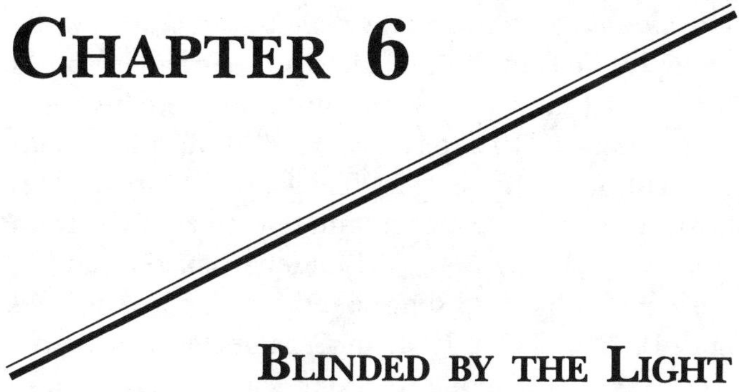

Chapter 6

Blinded by the Light

The Case of Betty Andreasson Luca

One of the most remarkable series of encounters with "alien" beings involves a devout Christian woman named Betty (Andreasson) Luca, her husband Bob Luca, and author Raymond E. Fowler (b. 1933 in Salem, Massachusetts). Fowler was the primary investigator of these paranormal encounters. All three claim to have been subjected to unusual experiences with otherworldly beings since childhood and also have witnessed numerous UFO sightings throughout their lives. Interestingly, under hypnosis all three attest to having been abducted at least once, but the focus of attention seems to be on Betty who, unfortunately, is the principal target of these entities and has been the victim of repeated abductions.

Coincidentally, Bob and Betty Luca, who met in the late 1970s and were married on 21 August 1978, each experienced a separate initial encounter with UFO entities in 1944 when they were children. Over twenty years later, in 1967, they both were individually abducted on different occasions and given some sort of medical examination. About two months after they were married in 1978, Bob and Betty were *simultaneously* abducted by "alien" creatures while living in Meriden, Connecticut. Of particular note is the fact that Bob's initial encounter with otherworldly beings back in 1944 also occurred in Meriden, Connecticut, when he was just five years old. In Bridgeport, Connecticut, approximately thirty-five miles southwest of Meriden, Al Bender's paranormal experiences with outer space beings took place in 1952 and 1953. Also in 1952 in Seaside Park, Milford, New Haven, and along the Long Island Sound (about twenty miles south of Meriden), numerous UFO sightings were reported. Between 8 and 19 August 1956 there was a concentration of UFO sightings approximately fifteen miles northeast of Meriden in and around Hartford, Connecticut.

Betty Andreasson Luca's case is well deserving of special attention not only because Betty claims to be a sincere Christian, but because of her entanglement with otherworldly beings. Her involvement, and the tactics employed on her by these beings, reveal many extraordinary similarities that occur with other UFO related contact cases. These significant, interconnected characteristics provide some very interesting clues which may enable us to uncloak the true source of the intelligence responsible for the multi-dimensional activities associated with the UFO phenomenon. In addition, her case is not only unique, but so fantastic that an in-depth evaluation of her experiences is essential to fully grasp the magnitude of the intellectual juggling that is taking place over her lifespan of adventures with these alien creatures.

There are more startling facts and circumstances involving the "alien" encounters of Betty Andreasson Luca and others that we will now investigate. Beginning in 1944 at the age of seven and continuing through 1989 at the age of 52, Betty Andreasson

Luca had at least fifteen different encounters with and/or abductions by otherworldly beings. Her experiences have been accurately and systematically documented by Raymond E. Fowler, who has written *The Andreasson Affair* (1979), *The Andreasson Affair, Phase Two* (1982), *The Watchers: The Secret Design Behind UFO Abduction* (1990), and *The Watchers II: Exploring UFOs and the Near Death Experience* (1995). Betty Andreasson Luca appears to be singled out by these entities. What can we learn from her experiences?

Over forty years of contact with what she thinks are benevolent extraterrestrials (or angelic beings) who belong to the "government of God" has resulted in Betty truly believing that she has been "chosen" to carry out a special mission. This mission, which has been implanted in her mind by these so-called extraterrestrials, is to bring to the population (the Christian population?) an awareness of these alien beings and their reason for visiting earth: ALIEN BEINGS FROM OUTER SPACE ARE NOW HERE TO HELP US!

We have heard this same scenario repeatedly from the extraterrestrials: We are here to help humanity. We are here to help humanity. We are here to help humanity. It is getting to be like a broken record. The contactees of the 1950s and 1960s informed us of this forty years ago. Today, New Age channelers, trance mediums, and disciples of the New Age movement, who are in telepathic communication with these entities, are also echoing these same preposterous messages. Just as in the case of Betty Andreasson Luca, there are other abductees who feel fortunate to be in contact with these otherworldly beings and are broadcasting these same kind-hearted messages.

In the last five decades, however, what have these so-called aliens actually done to help us? Where are they when we really need them? Who are these mysterious invaders, and why have they been covertly appearing and disappearing for over fifty years? What are their real intentions? The frightening truth is that these entities are, in fact, using humankind to help carry out their devious, yet undetected, mission.

Is Betty Andreasson Luca's "mission" an integral part of the overall "alien" strategy? Sadly, anyone who is in contact with otherworldly beings is involved (either knowingly or unknowingly) in the sinister, yet undisclosed, "alien" master plan. And, even more sadly, the contactees are being exploited and sifted like wheat.

Betty Andreasson Luca's repeated contacts with otherworldly beings seems very unsettling in light of the fact that she has strong Christian beliefs. But it is possible for a person, if he or she is sensitive to the spiritual realm, to misinterpret a visitation from otherworldly beings (as well as paranormal manifestations) as coming from God. Without realizing it, she could be involved in something *evil.* Has Betty succumbed to being deceived by these creatures? Has she been led to think that she is in contact with God's angelic messengers?

The Broader Connection

Assimilating the extraordinary connections between the phenomenon, the entities involved and their tactics employed on selected witnesses (including Betty Andreasson Luca) only serves to confirm the harsh reality that we are dealing with an intricately interwoven phenomenon. The fact that these complex similarities do indeed exist, however, may actually lead us to the point of origin and, in turn, to the intelligence responsible for these paranormal occurrences. A careful analysis reveals at least twenty-one specific correlations and key characteristics that are frequently present when certain humans encounter otherworldly entities (or have some type of paranormal experience), and/or intense UFO activity is evident in certain geographical locations, the following may occur:

1. One's telephone circuitry may malfunction.
2. An unpleasant odor may be present (like that of sulphur).
3. A blinding, bright light emanates from a UFO (or from some other unknown source) which has an intense effect on the witness. Other "strange" lights and/or flashes of light have also been reported.
4. One may experience paralysis (sometimes as a direct result of this bright light).
5. The witness may experience the sensation of floating, especially when being transported to or from the spaceship.
6. One may experience severe headaches (sometimes during and/or after a UFO experience).
7. The mutilation of animals often takes place in and around areas where UFOs have been reported.
8. The witness may be visited by three mysterious men wearing black clothing (known as the "Three Men in Black"). In some cases, these men resemble clergymen.
9. Mysterious accidents can occur resulting in injury and possible death of loved ones, friends, and the witnesses themselves.
10. During an abduction or contact experience, one may be given an oily liquid to drink. The

effects of this liquid cause the individual to relax. Sometimes an individual's entire body is "cleansed" with an oily liquid.

11. The "aliens" usually dress in uniforms (or tight-fitting one-piece suits) which often display some type of emblem.
12. The alien's eyes are described as strange, large, penetrating, hypnotic, and black with no pupils. In other instances, they are described as glowing or luminous.
13. During an abduction or contact experience, the aliens sometimes place black hoods over their own heads.
14. During an abduction or contact experience, an individual may encounter a *divine taller* being known as "the Exalted One," "the Old One," or simply "the One." This may result in some type of mystical, spiritual, or religious awakening for that individual.
15. During an abduction or contact experience, one may be subjected to some type of medical examination by the aliens while lying on a table. In some cases, during the examination, an eye-like scanning device descends from the ceiling and proceeds to examine the individual from head to toe. The aliens may extract urine, sperm, and other bodily fluids from the witness. Their most prized possession, however, is *blood.*
16. During the medical examination, females are often subjected to the insertion of a long needle into their naval.
17. During an abduction or contact experience, males are often forced to have sexual intercourse with supposed female alien beings.

18. During an abduction or contact experience, communication with alien beings often occurs via thought transference or telepathy.
19. After an abduction or contact experience, the subject may discover anomalous scars on his or her body. He or she may also be plagued by recurring nightmares and/or strange dreams. Many abductees and contactees undergo drastic personality changes following their paranormal experiences with alien entities.
20. After an abduction or contact experience, one may experience a loss of time in which he or she has no conscious memory of what has happened to them. Through a series of vivid dreams and/or nightmares, the contactee begins to recollect that something definitely strange occurred at some time in his or her life. Through hypnosis an individual can painstakingly recall his or her memories which have been suppressed in their unconscious mind.
21. Months or even years after an abduction or contact experience takes place, subjects often observe mysterious unmarked black helicopters flying over their homes.

The Betty Connection

Betty Andreasson Luca testified to many of these experiences during her encounters with masked invaders. The interaction of human individuals with "alien" beings can be very bizarre at times. In many instances, an individual's consciousness is raised to a higher spiritual, religious, or mystical plane. Betty's lifelong interactions with these otherworldly beings take on obviously "religious" overtones as demonstrated by the following list:

1. The "aliens" inform her that she has been given a special "blessing" in which she is told she would be *blessed above women.* (Perhaps like the Virgin Mary?)
2. Betty witnesses different types of "alien" beings. These beings somehow *transform themselves into beings of light.* (i.e., *Angels* of light?)
3. She is shown a "movie" (depicted on some type of viewing screen) involving a *church meeting.* Supposedly this is a church she attended when she was a young child in Ashburnham, Massachusetts. During this supposed *church meeting,* Betty recognizes the pastor who is speaking from a pulpit and his wife who appears to be reading the *Bible.* She also sees herself (as a child) along with her mother and father. Soon a *tall* alien being whispers something in the pastor's wife's ear. The pastor's wife then proceeds toward Betty and places her hands on Betty's head. The pastor's wife then begins to *speak in tongues.* Another *tall* "alien" entity places his hands on the minister's shoulders. The minister then interprets the strange dialect that is being spoken by his wife. Soon afterwards the minister also *speaks in tongues* (Fowler 1995).
4. On 25 January 1967 in South Ashburnham, Massachusetts, when Betty was thirty, she was abducted from her home by alien beings. At that time, she thought she was being visited by *angels.* She was then subjected to a physi-

cal examination and was taken to a mysterious other-worldly place where she witnessed the death and rebirth of a Phoenix-like bird. Interestingly enough, this Phoenix-like bird was also depicted in the emblems on the alien's uniforms. At this point, these alien beings told her that she had been specifically "*chosen*" to fulfill a particular "*mission.*" This mission was to communicate a message of such magnitude that it would eventually affect all of humanity (Fowler 1990).

5. During another abduction experience, Betty witnesses three *tall,* human-like "aliens" performing a strange, mystical ceremony which involves the triangular positioning of these three beings as they are seen standing within a circular symbol that has appeared on the floor. As they clasp the palms of their hands together, a circular ring of light appears in the center of them. Another beam of light emanates from their foreheads, thus forming a triangle. (*Another occult trinity?*) Soon after three other human-like beings join this unusual ritual by positioning themselves within this circular design on the floor where they all begin *chanting.* Another ring of light then appears and encircles the six of them (near the back of their heads). Then another beam of light emanates from the foreheads of the other three, forming another triangle. This creates two triangles, resulting in the configuration of a *six-pointed star.* They then proceed to raise their arms toward the sky, and the existing rays of light change into one globe of light (Fowler 1995).

The Practice of Magic

The six-pointed star, also known as the Double Triangle or the Sign or Seal of Solomon, is one of four geometrical diagrams used in the practice of *magic.* The other three are the Triangle (representing the trinity), the Tetragram (a four-pointed star), and the Pentagram (a five-pointed star). The Double Triangle (or the six-pointed star) represents the perfect number six. Magicians wear it during magical ceremonies. In fact, the geometrical designs of the Double Triangle, the Triangle, the Tetragram, and the Pentagram are of utmost importance when conjuring a spirit or *demon* by means of magical or supernatural powers. Circles with triangles drawn inside are generally drawn on the ground and particularly used by magicians during the evocation of certain spirits.

Magical ceremonies performed by magicians and witches indeed incorporate the ancient practice of *chanting.* The rhythmic vibrations caused by chanting during a magical ceremony play a vital role in the success of conjuring up invisible entities. Chanting can be traced back to the ancient Egyptians, who used similar rhythmic rituals to summon occult forces and/or powers. Another interesting fact is that the "Phoenix" (the particular bird that was shown to Betty during her 1967 abduction) is a legendary bird in Egyptian mythology that lived in the desert for five hundred years. After being consumed by fire, it rose from its own ashes, symbolizing death and resurrection.

The strange, mystical ceremony performed by alien beings (described by Betty Andreasson Luca) is remarkably similar to these magical ceremonies. By utilizing these geometrical magical diagrams (i.e., the circle, the triangle within the circle, and the six-pointed star) and the ancient ritual of chanting, these otherworldly beings appear to be performing some type of sorcerous, magical ceremony. Is this not a direct link to the occult?

Adam and Eve: An Extra-Biblical Source

The non-canonical work known as *The Forgotten Books of Eden* contains within it the apocryphal writings titled *The First Book of Adam and Eve* and *The Second Book of Adam and Eve*. These two books also are called *The Conflict of Adam and Eve with Satan*. While these books do not represent divinely inspired scriptures as contained in the canonical books of the Bible, as a body of religious literature akin to the Christian writings, they give an interesting and vivid description of the ever-changing forms of Satan and his hosts and their deceptive tactics on humankind. It is interesting to note that these descriptions bear a striking resemblance to the outer space entities described by Betty Andreasson Luca and others. Consider the following excerpts:

> After this Satan, the hater of good, took the form of an angel, and with him two others, so that they looked like the three angels who had brought to Adam gold, incense, and myrrh. Then Satan, the tallest of them, said, "Rejoice, O Adam, and be glad. Lo, God has sent us to thee to tell thee something."

—The thirteenth apparition of
Satan to Adam and Eve.
Book 1, chapter 70, vs. 1,5.

> Satan then appeared to him with thirty men of his hosts, in the form of handsome men; Satan

himself being the elder and tallest among them, with a fine beard.

—Book 2, chapter 17, v. 4.

Then Adam wept and said, "O God, remove us to some other place, that the serpent may not come again near us, and rise against us. Lest it find Thy handmaid Eve alone and kill her; for its eyes are hideous and evil."

—Book 1, chapter 20, v. 1.

When Satan, the hater of all good, saw how they continued in prayer, and how He had accepted their offering—Satan made an apparition. He began with transforming his hosts; in his hands was a flashing fire, and they were in a great light. And Satan did this, in order that when Adam saw the light, he should think within himself that it was a heavenly light, and that Satan's hosts were angels; and that God had sent them to watch at the cave, and to give him light in the darkness.

. . . This is Satan and his hosts; he wishes to deceive you at first. For the first time, he was hidden in the serpent; but this time he is come to you in the similitude of an angel of light; Then the angel went from Adam, and seized Satan at the opening of the cave, and stripped him of the feint he had assumed, and brought him in his own hideous form to Adam and Eve; who were afraid of him when they saw him. And the angel said to Adam, "This hideous form has been ever since God made him fall from heaven. He could not have come near you in it; therefore did he transform himself into an angel of light."

—The second tempting of Adam and Eve. The devil takes on the form of a beguiling light. Book 1, chapter 27, vs. 1,2,4,12-14.

But when the wily Satan saw them, that they were going to the garden, he gathered together his host, and came in appearance upon a cloud, intent on deceiving them. But when Adam and Eve saw him thus in a vision, they thought they were angels of God come to comfort them about their having left the garden, or to bring them back again into it.

—Book 1, chapter 28, vs. 1,2.

Then Satan, the hater of all good, envious of Adam and of his offering through which he found favor with God, hastened and took a sharp stone from among sharp iron-stones; appeared in the form of a man, and went and stood by Adam and Eve.

—Book 1, chapter 69, v. 1.

Then God ordered Satan to show himself to Adam plainly, in his own hideous form. But when Adam saw him, he feared, and trembled at the sight of him. And God said to Adam, "Look at this devil, and at his hideous look, and know that he it is who made thee fall from brightness into darkness, from peace and rest to toil and misery. And look, O Adam, at him, who said of himself that he is God! Can God be black? Would God take the form of a woman? Is there anyone stronger than God? And can He be overpowered? See, then, O Adam, and behold him bound in thy presence, in the air, unable to flee away! Therefore, I say unto thee, be not afraid of him; henceforth take care, and beware of him, in whatever he may do to thee."

—Book 2, chapter 4, vs. 1-5.

The Bible Tells Me So

Furthermore, the canonical scriptures of the Bible sufficiently illuminate us concerning the actions of the Devil (or Satan):

> And there was a war in heaven: Michael and his angels fought against the dragon; and the dragon fought and his angels, And prevailed not; neither was their place found any more in heaven. And the great dragon was cast out, that old serpent, called the Devil, and Satan, which deceiveth the whole world: he was cast out into the earth, and his angels were cast out with him.
>
> (Rev. 12:7-9)

> Wherein in time past ye walked according to the course of this world, according to the prince of the power of the air, the spirit that now worketh in the children of disobedience.
>
> (Eph. 2:2)

> And the Lord said unto Satan, From whence comest thou? And Satan answered the Lord, and said, From going to and fro in the earth, and from walking up and down in it.
>
> (Job 2:2)

Thus, according to the Bible, *Satan* and his host of fallen angels (or *demons*) occupy the earth (and the air that surrounds the earth). Apparently, they can assume any shape or form for the purpose of deceiving humankind, including the ability to imitate angelic or spiritual beings (cf., II Cor. 11:13-15). Is it not within the realm of possibility that *Satan* and his host of *demons* are now posing as extraterrestrials? If by chance we were to encounter these so-called alien beings from another world (and it is highly unlikely that this contact would occur by chance), would we be able to, from a Christian standpoint, test the spirits (or aliens)? The Bible, in fact, instructs us on how to test the spirits:

> Beloved, believe not every spirit, but try the spirits whether they are of God: because many false prophets are gone out into the world. Hereby know ye the Spirit of God: Every spirit that confesseth that Jesus Christ is come in the flesh is of God: And every spirit that confesseth not that Jesus Christ is come in the flesh is not of God: and this is that spirit of antichrist, whereof ye have heard that it should come; and even now already is it in the world.
>
> (I John 4:1-3)

Of particular note is that during Betty's abduction experience on 25 January 1967, after witnessing the death and rebirth of the Phoenix-like bird, she began to converse with a loud voice. During her conversation with this voice, she explicitly asks the voice these three significant questions:

1. Are you God?
2. Are you the Lord God?
3. Are you my Lord Jesus?

At no time did this voice answer yes.

The Extraterrestrial Link

In the previous five chapters, an objective presentation of the mystifying facts has unfolded that intricately connects the UFO phenomenon with various religious, New Age, and occult doctrines and organizations. It has also been proposed that Satan and his host of demons may, in fact, be posing as extraterrestrials. Are they, therefore, manifesting themselves as extraterrestrials to certain human individuals? Could we be encountering the same supernatural deities that exerted an evil influence on Solomon and the children of Israel three thousand years ago?

Psychological Warfare

It is difficult to imagine the extent of the conditioning process that is at work within the UFO phenomenon. It pervades virtually every level of our society as we know it. And, particularly as we approach the twenty-first century, the entire human population is being conditioned to accept the deluded notion that an extraterrestrial race exists and that these extraterrestrials are now making contact with earth.

One wonders why it has not become evident to more people that a *sinister* intelligence does exist and is cleverly and cunningly at work behind an "alien" smoke screen, concealing its actual intentions. In order to achieve the primary goal, this insidious intelligence is manipulating key people on earth, either directly or indirectly. Through an ingenious process, these key individuals are accepting an entirely new belief system and, in turn, influencing our established religious, political, and social structures. Through the "channels" of our technological advancements (i.e., television, radio, motion pictures, computers, the Internet, etc.), these new beliefs are becoming accepted instantly as fact by thousands of people the world over.

How long will it be before this crafty intelligence accomplishes its overall secret agenda, before everyone believes in UFOs and accepts these "aliens" as our extraterrestrial saviors?

It is plausible that UFO sightings, UFO contacts with alien beings, and telepathic communications with so-called outer space entities are all part and parcel of a deceptive masterminded plan. The driving, motivating force behind this plan, as mentioned, is to condition and deceive the entire population into thinking we are now being visited by a superior extraterrestrial civilization. This conditioning process is, therefore, brainwashing humanity which, in turn, is promoting the universal acceptance of "extraterrestrial" intervention here on earth. As this conditioning process continues, a very dangerous and malicious force is presently and continually at work fulfilling its desired mission.

This universal acceptance of "alien" intervention will ultimately and drastically change our sociopolitical and socio-religious systems. Its repercussions are already being felt in our society today. Millions of people across the globe are anxiously awaiting the first public landings of so-called extraterrestrial spaceships. And, supposedly, on board are benevolent extraterrestrial beings who possess intergalactic wisdom and the necessary knowledge needed to help guide us into the twenty-first century. Are millions of people being led to place their faith and hope in unidentified extraterrestrial saviours from outer space?

This expectation has already manifested itself when, in the fall of 1996, a rumor began circulating that an alien spacecraft will make a public landing somewhere in the southwestern United States between 1997 and the year 2000 (near Roswell?). Soon after this momentous event occurs, numerous other alien spaceships will land, undoubtedly sparking worldwide publicity. Amazingly (so the rumor goes), the United States government, military, and certain world leaders, including the President of the United States, have already been informed of this spectacular event. It is no surprise that these powerful organizations and ruling individuals claim to already know who the extraterrestrials are and where they come from. Are the "aliens" and the United States government working together covertly? Or is the United States government, in fact, concocting this fantastic scheme?

It is an established fact that the entire population has been conditioned via television (and other forms of communication) to think that we are in contact with extraterrestrials. So, an "official" landing would not be a surprise. In actuality, the masses are being readied for such an occurrence. Unfortunately, entire segments of humanity are unwittingly accepting an erroneous belief system. The "extraterrestrial" psychological warfare that has been waged against us since the 1940s by, in all likelihood, human and alien sinister forces is advancing right on schedule.

Is the United States government, along with certain powerful and influential world leaders, responsible for this psychological warfare? Or is the government being manipulated by the UFO phenomenon itself? What if the U.S. government, in fact, cunningly staged what appears to be an "alien landing" and, in so doing, used this spectacular, devious performance for their own ulterior motives? Could its motives even be playing into the hands of the "aliens" and serving a grander scheme? Will it ever be possible to uncover the full truth amid this global cloak-and-dagger activity?

The formative years of the movement are now over. Its rapid advances are frightening. It has become apparent that a unique stratagem is at work on this planet, targeting the human *mind.* This mission is being undertaken by skilled, masked invaders who do not really reside on the planet Mars or Venus or any other planet. These invaders are, in fact, the initiators of this ingenious, yet deceptive, *supernatural* operation. The genius of this operation has been the formation of a world network over this past century. These invaders, who many now believe are our extraterrestrial saviors, have been spoon-feeding key individuals, resulting in the propagation of a bogus intergalactic gospel of salvation to humankind. Has the United States government (along with certain powerful world leaders) been in contact with these so-called extraterrestrials? Is it possible that a few high-ranking U.S. government officials, along with some of our key world leaders, have a pact with these "alien" beings in exchange for secret interstellar information?

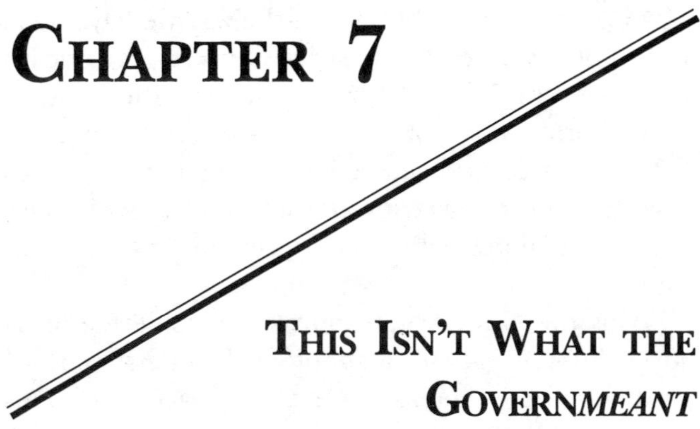

Chapter 7

This Isn't What the Govern*meant*

> I pledge allegiance to the flag of the United States of America; and to the Republic for which it stands, one Nation under God, indivisible, with liberty and justice for all.

Every morning when my seven-year-old son goes to school, he and his classmates recite the "Pledge of Allegiance." Over thirty years ago when I was in school, I also recited "The Pledge." In fact, millions of Americans have recited this solemn pledge to the United States for over one hundred years. There is no doubt in my mind that this is a great country. I personally would not want to live anywhere else, and I assume this is likely the feeling of most American citizens. Are we truly a nation under God, though? Do we as a nation embrace Christian values and morals? Are our most powerful government officials always straightforward with the American public? For undisclosed reasons, could they be carrying out manipulative and deceptive maneuvers?

Crash Go the Saucers

As previously stated in chapter two, the United States government is intricately involved with the

UFO phenomenon, but not in the way we have been led to believe. For the past few decades, Americans have been brainwashed by the media with accounts of elaborate tales of "crashed saucers" and dead "aliens." It is also alleged that the United States government has retrieved the wreckage of these spacecraft along with their deceased "alien" occupants.

Has the United States government developed a super-human "alien" technology from its years of studying these "aliens" and their spaceships? Has this technology, in turn, enabled them to unlock the mysteries of the universe? It is questionable. But this is certainly what they want us to *think.* If *we, the people* of the United States, are led to believe that our government has actually recovered "alien beings," as well as fragments of their spacecraft, it only serves to magnify their "power" base. This position of superiority generates a false belief system which, in turn, complicates many UFO investigations and manipulates the tide of the public opinion. Our attention, therefore, is diverted to incredible accounts of "crashed saucers," rather than being informed of actual (and suppressed) UFO incidents that are continually taking place. We are being led to suspect that the United States government possesses some remarkably superior alien technology. While this is highly unlikely, the possibility that the United States military is manufacturing and testing UFO-type craft should not be ruled out.

For the record, the following list contains the presumed locations and dates of the most popular alleged alien spaceship crashes:

1. Roswell, New Mexico, 4 July 1947
2. Magdalena, New Mexico, 5 July 1947
3. Kingman, Arizona, 21 May 1953

4. Ubatuba, Brazil, 14 September 1957
5. Las Vegas, Nevada, 18 April 1962
6. Kecksburg, Pennsylvania, 9 December 1965

The fact remains that in all of these supposed "alien" spaceship crashes, there is not one piece of solid physical evidence to support the notion that something "alien" actually crashed. Curiously, however, during the 1990s, certain UFO investigators anonymously received supposed fragments from the 1947 Roswell crash. Who is trying to keep the crashed saucer soap opera alive? And for what purpose? Why all this disinformation and misinformation? Is the United States government responsible for such devious actions?

Earth vs. the Flying Saucers

Back in the 1940s and 1950s, when UFO (i.e., flying saucer) sightings were being reported at an alarming rate throughout the world, the United States and other governments were, in all likelihood, baffled and intrigued by the possibility that "extraterrestrials" were visiting the earth. Naturally, the immediate concern was the security of their own nations and the planet as a whole. Each nation began investigating the overwhelming UFO phenomenon and rallying their own military defenses. In 1952 the United States Air Force appointed an investigation committee called Project Blue Book. In 1969 after 17 years of investigative research, Project Blue Book was deactivated. The committee concluded that there was no evidence of a UFO threat to our national security.

The Navy Contact: Frances Swan

Worth noting is the experience of contactee Frances Swan of Eliot, Maine (mentioned in chapters two and three), who lived next to a retired Navy admiral named Herbert B. Knowles. On 18 May 1954 during a specific contact via automatic writing with Affa from Uranus, Affa instructed Swan to contact the Navy and inform them that they would be able to receive outer space messages via radio communications. Naturally, Swan thought of her neighbor, Admiral Knowles. She immediately decided to reveal to him and his wife Helen that she was in contact with outer space beings.

These spectacular allegations triggered a series of investigations involving certain military and government personnel, including members of the Office of Naval Intelligence (ONI), the Navy's Bureau of Aeronautics, the Central Intelligence Agency, and Project Blue Book. During these investigations, it was reported that Affa, in fact, had communicated with certain military personnel via automatic writing. It was also reported that following these investigations, Swan secretly worked with certain members of various U.S. intelligence groups while receiving daily messages from numerous outer space entities. What specific messages were these entities transmitting to Frances Swan and to these U.S. intelligence personnel of the United States government? Is the United States government presently communicating with so-called extraterrestrials via channeling, automatic writing, and the ouija board?

It is not surprising that the Swan situation caused an immediate stir among certain government and military organizations. Here was an ideal opportunity to satisfy their curiosity and communicate with supposed alien beings from another planet through Mrs. Swan.

What ever became of Frances Swan? Does she still work for the U.S. government? Is the U.S. government currently hiring New Age "channelers" and psychics who are in contact with supposed extraterrestrial beings?

Ouija In the White House?

It has been reported that First Lady Hillary Clinton (born 1947 in Chicago, Illinois) frequently confers with spiritualist medium and psychic Jean Houston. Jean Houston claims to be in contact with a spirit entity named Athena (the ancient Greek goddess). Athena, if you recall from chapters three and four, is currently a female commander of the Starship of Sananda and one of four associates involved with the Ashtar Command. This raises an important question: Are the Clintons communicating with supposed alien beings of the Ashtar Command? Could Ashtar be influencing the President of the United States?

Presidential Candidate: Gabriel Green

As highlighted in chapter four, contactee Gabriel Green channels messages from various outer space beings, including members of the Ashtar Command. The web is further weaved by the fact that he was asked by a particular "extraterrestrial" (Ashtar?) to run for President of the United States back in 1960. He campaigned for a short while under an independent party but eventually withdrew in support of John F. Kennedy. Two years later, in 1962, Green ran for U.S. Senate from California and received 171,000 votes. He was endorsed by Linus Pauling (born 28 February 1901 in Portland, Oregon), an American chemist who won the 1954 Nobel prize and the 1963 Nobel Peace Prize.

Ten years later, in 1972, Green again ran for President of the United States under the Universal

Party, formed by contactee Daniel Fry (mentioned in chapter two), Green's vice-presidential running mate. The Universal Party offered the American people solutions to national and international problems proposed by extraterrestrial beings via outer space contact. These advanced extraterrestrial beings also influenced Green in supporting the economics of a cashless society, a system supposedly in use on other planets. Is President Bill Clinton (William Jefferson Blythe III, born 1946 in Hope, Arkansas) now following in the footsteps of Gabriel Green thirty years later?

The Future's Money System

Today as we witness the rapid growth of a one-world economy and the institution of a "New World Order," the cashless society envisioned by Gabriel Green (and Bill Clinton?) is racing towards reality. Paper money and coins touting "In God We Trust" will soon be obsolete. "Mondex" Money, or plastic cards which act as a cash substitute, is already being test-marketed.

In the not-too-distant future, all bank transactions will be done by telephone or computer. There will be no tellers. Money will be digital. Savings account earnings will be counted by the number of microscopic dots on a personal electronic computer chip. This digital money then can be easily electronically monitored by the U.S. Treasury, the Federal Reserve, and the Internal Revenue Service.

Remote Viewing

It would come as no surprise if the U.S. government, in fact, had in its arsenal a secret group of "psychic" individuals who are in communion with so-called extraterrestrials. It has already been reported that for the past twenty years, U.S. government intelligence groups, namely the CIA, have been working with gifted psychics known as "remote viewers." These extraordinary people claim that they not only have the ability to observe future events, but can actually travel great distances (by leaving their body) and survey present events at the distant location. For example, a remote viewer could be out of his or her body at this precise moment, visiting you while you are in your living room, and watching you as you read this book! Now, there is not only easy surveillance on the activity of your bank account, but surveillance occurring in the privacy of your own home.

It is interesting to note that Betty Andreasson Luca traveled to some mysterious realm while having an out of body experience and encountered otherworldly beings. Are these remote viewers, or anyone else who leaves their body for that matter, entering the same etheric plane that *demons* inhabit? Do otherworldly beings (or demons) inhabit a parallel universe that exists in the ethereal realm of the earth's atmosphere?

All I Need Is the Air That I Breathe . . .

The earth's atmosphere consists of five separate regions or layers, each containing a mixture of various gases and having different temperatures. We live in the first region called the *troposphere,* which extends approximately five to ten miles above the earth's surface. The second region or layer is called the *stratosphere* and extends approximately thirty miles above the troposphere. Above the stratosphere and extending approximately fifty miles above the earth's surface lies the *mesosphere.* The *thermosphere,* which exists above the mesophere, reaches about four hundred miles into space, and temperatures steadily increase with altitude. The *exosphere* is the outermost layer of the earth's atmosphere and extends thousands of miles into space.

The first three layers of the earth's atmosphere (i.e., troposphere, stratosphere, and mesosphere) contain mostly nitrogen and oxygen. The sun's ultraviolet rays interact with the oxygen in the stratosphere, chemically changing its atomic structure to form ozone. A high concentration of ozone, known as the ozone layer, exists approximately twelve to thirty miles above the earth's surface in the stratosphere. Ozone is an essential ingredient in our atmosphere because it filters out damaging ultraviolet radiation that can penetrate our planet.

In 1985 a group of scientists discovered that a section of the ozone layer above Antarctica was being depleted. Eight years later, in 1993, it was detected that this "hole" had expanded to about the size of North America, reaching southern parts of South America and Australia. It is also known that numerous smaller "holes" exist around the circumference of the planet (as if somebody fired a shotgun), including sections above the United States. Industrial chemicals, such as chlorofluorocarbons and carbon tetrachloride, are believed to be the cause of the depletion. But, are they the *major* cause?

Honey, I Blew Up the Atmosphere

Some crazed U.S. scientist during the 1950s theorized that by exploding a nuclear bomb in the earth's atmosphere, he could change the earth's magnetic field, thus creating a layer of artificial radiation that would destroy enemy satellites. It was reported that in August and September of 1958, several nuclear bombs were detonated in the earth's atmosphere approximately 125 to 300 miles above the earth's surface over the south Atlantic Ocean near Antarctica (Keith 1994). Could these nuclear explosions be responsible for the "hole" in the ozone layer? Unfortunately, four years later, in 1962, this experiment was repeated by the Soviets over Siberia.

Is the constant depletion of the ozone layer the culprit in the case of the ill-health of millions of people around the globe? Are we, in fact, being radiated? Is this dose of radiation having a detrimental effect on our minds as well? Could this be, in part, responsible for the senseless, mindless, horrible murders that are taking place throughout the world at an alarming rate? Or is the U.S. government actually test-marketing an advanced technological weapon capable of distorting our minds and altering our thought processes?

The World According To HAARP

Today, six rows of six large, super-powerful radio antennas point toward the sky in Gakona, Alaska. This project, known as the High-frequency Active Auroral Research Program, or HAARP, is the most powerful radio transmitter ever built in the world. HAARP is managed jointly by the U.S. Air Force and the U.S. Navy, along with the University of Alaska. This advanced scientific research center is experimenting with the earth's atmosphere. These powerful antennas are sending out radio signals into the ionosphere causing electromagnetic waves to bounce back toward earth (Begich 1996). For what purpose? What effect will this have on humanity?

The Department of Defense declares that HAARP research is developing an advanced technology that will replace existing U.S. military communications and radar systems. This new technology will also enable the military to neutralize foreign communications in specific geographical areas without interfering with its own communications (Begich 1996). This is all fine and dandy when it comes to our national security, but could HAARP somehow be damaging the ionosphere as well?

Let's Get Radiated

The *ionosphere* is located in the thermosphere (i.e., the fourth layer of the earth's atmosphere approximately fifty to four hundred miles above the earth's surface). It contains a high concentration (or layer) of electrically charged atoms or molecules known as ions. This layer of ions in the ionosphere normally reflects radio waves and radio signals. The chemical makeup of the ionosphere also blocks harmful radiation coming from the sun that can penetrate our planet. An alarming prospect is that federal reports indicate that HAARP plans to alter the chemical composition of the ionosphere for its military defense purposes. By altering the ionosphere, the military can achieve its strategic goal by utilizing various invisible radiation waves of the electromagnetic spectrum (i.e., the entire range of radiation extending in frequency by wavelengths).

Two very unsettling question emerge: Is HAARP altering the chemical balance of the ionosphere to the point of enabling harmful solar radiation to penetrate the earth? And are we now being radiated by (1) the depletion of the ozone layer, (2) the altering of the chemical composition of the ionosphere, and (3) the direct result of the U.S. military's new defense technology known as HAARP?

As previously mentioned, HAARP antennas actually transmit radio waves into the ionosphere causing electromagnetically radiated energy to bounce back toward earth. Unfortunately, large doses of electromagnetic energy aimed at the earth can produce severe negative physiological effects on the human mind. An individual or a group of individuals (such as a whole country) can be placed in a temporary (or permanent) state of confusion, not knowing who they are or where they are as a result of being zapped by these electromagnetic beams of energy (Begich 1996).

The Electromagnetic Spectrum

Actually, there are many different types of electromagnetic radiation. All radiant energy, or energy that is transferred by electromagnetic radiation, exists in the form of electromagnetic waves. These waves can be hundreds of miles long or as short as a billionth of an inch. Beginning with the longest electromagnetic waves, the various types of electromagnetic radiation are:

1. Alternating current (i.e., AC from generators)
2. Radio waves (i.e., long-wave radio broadcasting or short-wave radio broadcasting)
3. Microwaves (i.e., microwave ovens; radar; cellular telephones)
4. Infrared radiation (i.e., thermal or heat radiation)
5. Visible light (i.e., visible radiant energy)
6. Ultraviolet radiation (i.e., radiation from the sun, which can cause sun burn and skin cancer)
7. X-Rays (i.e., penetrating photons used in radiology and radiotherapy)
8. Gamma rays (i.e., radiation emitted by radioactive decay; radium)

9. Cosmic rays (i.e., ionizing radiation from outer space)

Thus, this list illustrates the various forms of electromagnetic energy that exist in the electromagnetic spectrum. Visible light, which is located approximately in the center of the electromagnetic spectrum, makes up about three percent of the electromagnetic waves found in the electromagnetic spectrum. This leaves the remaining ninety-seven percent of electromagnetic radiation that exists above and below visible light invisible to the human eye. The exploitation of this invisible electromagnetic radiation by the U.S. military for defense purposes is the prime function of HAARP. Is the U.S. military, in fact, designing the perfect geophysical weapon? Is moving underground the only way to avoid being radiated?

An Underground Movement

In 1949 President Harry S. Truman (1884-1972) ordered the construction of an underground facility near Camp David. Now known as the "Underground Pentagon," this 265,000 square foot chamber lies well protected under 650 feet of granite. In fact, it has been reported that there are approximately fifty other underground military installations throughout the United States capable of housing thousands of individuals (Keith 1994). Evidently, the U.S. government has already taken great pains to protect itself from this vast amount of radiation poisoning that is now penetrating our planet. Could the U.S. government also be exploding nuclear bombs under the earth's surface in order to "hollow out" large areas for the sole purpose of constructing these underground facilities?

From 31 May 1987 to October 1994, Puerto Rico has been the target of intense underground explosions resulting in unusual earthquakes (Corrales 1995). Could the U.S. military be responsible for these underground detonations? Coincidently, over thirty percent of the island has been taken over by U.S. military bases. Ironically, these explosions began to occur after an alleged crash of an "alien" spaceship near the El Yunque rainforest, underneath which many of these explosions seem to occur (Corrales 1995). Did the U.S. military stage a UFO crash in the El Yunque rainforest, thus making it appear like "aliens" are to blame for these underground explosions?

It is interesting to note that numerous caves already exist under the island of Puerto Rico. Is the U.S. government exploiting these caves and enlarging them by exploding nuclear bombs for the purpose of constructing other subterranean military installations?

Spirit-Inhabited Atmosphere?

Demons, as spirit beings, coexist on a spiritual plane that apparently occupies the same physical space as our universe. Jesus engaged demons "face to face" on numerous occasions (cf., Mark 1:23-27; 5:1-15; 9:17-25). The apostle Paul augments the biblical reality by referring to the abode of the demons as the "air" (cf., Eph. 2:2), the "heavenlies" (i.e., "sky"), and even "not flesh and blood" (cf., Eph. 6:12).

While the Bible makes it clear that such demon entities are eternal and incapable of being annihilated (cf., Matt. 25:41; Rev. 20:10), perhaps the Satanic "master plan" includes duping humanity into believing that "extraterrestrials" exist and their concern is that we are upsetting the balance of the universe by our frequent nuclear detonations and the altering of the chemical composition of the ionosphere. After all, Satan is a schemer (cf., II Cor. 2:11; Eph. 6:11) and a bearer of many disguises (cf., II Cor. 11:14). The demons, also, are capable of performing signs to impress humans (cf., Rev. 16:13-14)!

This plan may even include unearthing unusual "creatures" that violently interact with the human and animal kingdom. This is certainly not beyond the capabilities of the *arch* deceiver (See Rev. 9:1-11).

CHAPTER 8

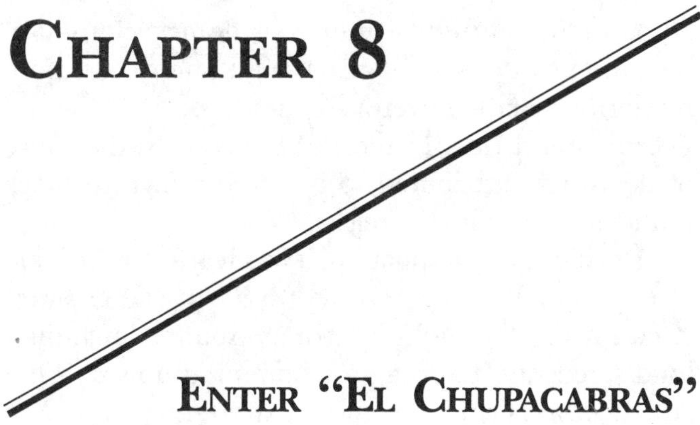

ENTER "EL CHUPACABRAS"

Mysterious Mutilations

During the past few decades, residents of Puerto Rico have reported seeing mysterious creatures roaming the countryside. On the night of 31 March 1991 while inside their home in Palmarejo, Puerto Rico, a husband and wife heard an unusual sound outside. Their two dogs, male and female Dobermans, were outside in the yard when they began barking and howling (apparently disturbed by the peculiar sound). The husband, after hearing a yelp followed by a sudden silence, decided to investigate. He was startled by two strange, gray beings, approximately three and a half feet tall with large heads and large black eyes, who quickly ran away when they saw him. The man then began looking for his dogs. He was relieved to find the female unharmed, but sad and outraged to discover that the male suffered a gruesome, sinister fate. Its eye sockets were empty, and apparently all of its internal organs were missing. Shocked and devastated, he surmised that his dog's insides had been sucked out through its eyes.

Sixteen years earlier in 1975, Puerto Rico was plagued by a series of unexplained animal deaths, all occurring at night. Numerous domestic animals, including cattle, sheep, goats, pigs, and ducks, were mysteriously killed over a six month period between February and July. In most of these cases, the cause of death was attributed to a severe puncture mark found in the animals' necks.

During the investigation, it was learned that some of the animal owners testified to having been awakened during the night by strange sounds, including loud screeches, flapping, or humming noises. What adds to the eeriness of these experiences is that in and around the vicinity of these mystifying animal deaths, there were reports of large, unidentified birds, as well as numerous UFO sightings.

The Goat Suckers

Beginning in the spring of 1995 and continuing through 1996, Puerto Rico once again fell prey to a series of mysterious animal deaths. Hundreds of goats, sheep, cattle, chickens, dogs, cats, hens and other farm animals were found mutilated and drained of their *blood.* This has created quite a stir, and it has been reported that a vampire-like animal is responsible for these killings. This enigmatic creature has been dubbed "the *chupacabras*" (which means "goat sucker" in Spanish).

Various descriptions of the chupacabras have run the gamut, as is noted below:

1. Body: Bipedal. Covered with coarse hair (usually black). One row of red-colored "spikes" or feathers running down its back. Tail/no tail. Wings/no wings.
2. Height: Three to four feet.
3. Color: It appears to have the ability to change colors (i.e., black, brown, green, or gray), depending on its surroundings.

4. Head: Oval, with an elongated jaw.
5. Eyes: Two, very large and slanted. Glowing red at night. Dark gray, black or red during the day.
6. Mouth: Slit-like with long, pointed teeth.
7. Ears: Small and pointed.
8. Arms: Two, with claw-like hands containing three digits (with long nails).
9. Legs: Two hind, with claw-like feet containing three digits (with long nails).

In some instances, witnesses have alleged that the chupacabras can either fly, rise straight up in the air, leap great distances, or appear luminous.

It is intriguing that small puncture holes have also been found in the necks of these animals supposedly mutilated by the chupacabras. In numerous animals, these puncture holes penetrated the cerebellum of the brain, causing instant death and very little suffering on the part of the animal. Also, certain organs seem to have been "surgically" removed from their bodies. Apparently, this creature exhibits extreme "intelligence" (Martin, Jorge 1996).

Native town folk who have actually seen the chupacabras report that an unpleasant *odor,* similar to sulphur, seems to exude from the creature. In a surprising twist of fate, these people have also witnessed numerous UFO sightings in and around the geographic locations where the chupacabras are being reported.

Alien Intervention?

An interesting fact is that UFO sightings have been reported in Puerto Rico since the early 1970s. Of particular note is that there was a major UFO flap in 1972 and 1973 and strange "men in black" were seen strolling down the streets. Also, there were numerous reports of people "missing" during those rather unusual years, which were characterized by much storytelling.

The decade of the 1990s heralded yet another resurgence of the UFO phenomenon in Puerto Rico. Numerous UFO sightings, abductions, and encounters with "alien" entities have escalated at an alarming rate. With the addition of the chupacabras attacks (associated with hundreds of animal mutilations), many are linking this frightening creature to the UFO phenomenon. Are the chupacabras, in fact, just another manifestation of our *supernatural* UFO entities? Do these vampire-like beings need human or animal *blood* in order to transmogrify? (To transmogrify is to change into a different shape or form, especially one that is fantastic or bizarre.)

Apparently more than one creature is involved since Puerto Rico is not the only host to chupacabras attacks. Witnesses in Mexico, Costa Rica, Guatemala, Brazil, Peru, and parts of the southern United States have equally reported strange creatures and cases of variously mutilated animals.

It is worth noting that during the decade of the 1990s, numerous UFO sightings have been reported in the aforementioned countries, particularly Mexico, Brazil, Puerto Rico, and the southern United States. The San Luis Valley region (southern Colorado and northern New Mexico, mentioned in chapter four) and Florida have witnessed repeated UFO activity during the 1980s and 1990s. A fact not generally advertised is that since the 1960s, the San Luis Valley area has simultaneously reported numerous UFO sightings and unusual animal mutilations. In addition, the United States, Brazil, and Mexico have witnessed thousands of UFO sightings and numerous UFO "flaps" since the late 1940s.

Mysterious Infant Deaths

In Mexico during the late 1970s, there were disturbing reports of mysterious deaths involving newborn babies. These infants were found with their tiny bodies literally drained of *blood.* In most cases, marks resembling hematomas were discovered on their skin, suggesting that their blood was sucked out through their skin. In the remaining instances, it appeared that the blood was sucked out through the infants' mouths (Freixedo 1996). Who or what could have been responsible for these horrible, loathsome acts? Is it not reasonable to assume that something *unearthly* could have been responsible?

A common occurrence worth noting is that in nearly every case where these lifeless babies were discovered, their mothers were found alongside them in some kind of inexplicable state of unconsciousness resembling a deep sleep. Some of these mothers did not wake up until days later (only to sadly discover the gruesome fate of their child). It should also be pointed out that in and around the vicinity where these unspeakable deaths occurred, numerous strange, nocturnal lights were witnessed in the nearby sky by the local townspeople (Freixedo 1996). Are there supernatural vampire-like entities from outer space sucking the blood out of innocent, helpless, newborn babies? Are the glowing red eyes of these "alien beings" hypnotizing young mothers into a deep sleep while the aliens replenish their veins with human blood?

Mothman

Approximately ten years earlier, from 1966 through 1967 during the Ohio River Valley/West Virginia UFO flap that targeted Point Pleasant, West

Virginia (mentioned in chapter five), farm animals, such as cows, horses, and particularly dogs, were found mutilated and *bloodless*, with visible wounds to their throats. Similarly, a dark, five to seven foot tall, human-like, winged creature with large, red-glowing, "hypnotic" eyes (known as *Mothman*) was repeatedly seen by more than one hundred people (Keel 1975b).

Coincidence?

Certainly it is not just a coincidence that numerous UFO sightings, animal mutilations, and reports of strange creatures (with glowing red eyes) are occurring simultaneously in and around the same geographical locations. Is it not plausible that these mind-boggling, coincidental occurrences are, in fact, somehow interconnected? History has bequeathed us numerous reports of strange, mystifying, *unearthly* creatures. In some cases, these creatures can be tied to certain mysterious human and animal deaths. Some may even be linked to UFOs. The following list has been compiled in an attempt to unscramble the plethora of associations that some of these creatures have had with common names, descriptions, geographical locations, dates, victims, and nature of deaths:

1. "Black Dogs:" These are huge, *supernatural* (or vanishing) black dogs with "glowing" eyes (usually "red"): France, A.D. 856; England, 1577 (these dogs attacked humans worshipping in a *church* resulting in death and/or injury); United States, Mississippi, 1930s; Pennsylvania, 1950s; South Africa, 1963 (associated with a UFO sighting); England, 1969, 1972; United States, Georgia, 1973 (associ-

ated with a UFO sighting); England, 1974; Devonshire, England, *Halloween,* 1984.

2. "The Beast of Gevaudan:" (i.e., "Werewolf") In France, between 1764 and 1767, sixty humans, particularly *children,* were mutilated and slaughtered.
3. "Bigfoot" or "Sasquatch:" A large, hairy, bipedal, nocturnal, ape-like creature: northwestern United States and western Canada, 1800s, 1900s.
4. "The Crawfordsville Monster:" A large (20 feet long and 8 feet wide), horrible, headless "thing" hovering in the air with flapping fins and a "flaming red" eye: Crawfordsville, Indiana, 5-6 September 1891.
5. "The Jersey Devil:" A winged, black, hideous-looking, cloven-hoofed creature, approximately four feet tall with glowing eyes: New Jersey, Pennsylvania, 16-23 January 1909. Also, numerous chickens were found dead with no marks on them.
6. "The Flatwoods Monster" (mentioned in chapter two): A huge, scary creature (approximately ten feet tall) with an "ace of spades" shaped head and two glowing eyes: Flatwoods, West Virginia, 12 September 1952 (associated with a UFO sighting). One week earlier, in Weston, West Virginia, approximately ten miles from Flatwoods, a similar looking creature was reportedly seen by two women. Both the "Flatwoods monster" and the creature seen in Weston emitted a foul odor. On 22 November 1973 a similar creature was also reported by a woman in Quebec, Canada.
7. "The Beast (or Beasts) of Exmoor:" Huge, black or tan cats and large, strange animals

resembling dogs were seen in England through the 1970s, 1980s, and 1990s and reported as having ripped the throats out of hundreds of sheep (Devonshire, England, 1983).

8. "Momo:" A tall, black, hairy, half-ape, half-human creature with a putrid odor, reported in northeastern Missouri in July 1971 and July 1972 (associated with numerous UFO sightings).
9. "Big Bird:" A huge, gruesome, black bird with a man's head and red eyes was spotted in Texas from November 1975 through January 1976.
10. "The Dover Demon:" A creature approximately four feet tall with an oversized, elongated head, long fingers, and glowing red or green eyes: sighted in Dover (Boston), Massachusetts, 21-22 April 1977.

It should be pointed out that these are some of the more popular among literally thousands of reports of bizarre creatures from all over the world dating back hundreds and even thousands of years. Do these creatures originate from a supernatural dimension? There are numerous reports that include strange creatures vanishing into thin air.

As previously stated, these mysterious creatures are also associated with unusual nocturnal lights and UFOs. Are the true forms of these hideous UFO entities monster-like? (The reader is reminded of the cases of Al Bender, John Stuart and J.D. "Sonny" Desvergers and their confrontations with hideous monsters noted in chapter two.) Are these *supernatural* creatures *demonic,* malevolent spirits and if so, are they occupying the earth and transforming themselves into physical beings for some undisclosed purpose? Do these entities need *blood* to replenish themselves or to transform themselves into "human-like" or other physical forms?

Monsters From the Netherworld?

The study of malevolent spirits that supposedly occupy the earth (or the ethereal realm that surrounds the earth) is the occult science Demonology. Thousands of years ago, ancient cultures attempted to record the experiences of certain humans who were pursued by or influenced by certain *evil* spirits. Demonology is regarded by occultists as a branch of magic in which certain spirits are conjured up and subsequently worshipped. These spirits were named *demons.* Demons are generally considered by Christians to be fallen angels, which are those beings that left their first estate as angelic hosts originally created by God.

In the Bible's New Testament book of Revelation, chapter twelve, we learn that a spiritual battle was fought in heaven. According to one Christian perspective, Lucifer (i.e., "light giver") was puffed up with pride and did not want to serve God, but wanted to be equal with God (cf., Isa. 14:13-14; I Tim. 3:6). This ambition of Lucifer provoked a rebellion against God and, in turn, one-third of God's angels rallied to Lucifer's support. Lucifer was opposed by the archangel Michael ("who is like unto God") along with the rest of God's angels, and there ensued a battle in which Michael was victorious. As a result, Lucifer and his host of fallen angels were cast out of heaven and consigned to hell (cf., Isa. 14:12-15). They are now referred to as the demons. However, even though Satan and his host of demons had been consigned to hell, they were first cast down to the earth (cf., Rev. 12:9). The Bible further illuminates us concerning the whereabouts of Satan:

> . . . Woe to the inhabiters of the earth and of the sea! for the devil is come down unto you, and having great wrath, because he knoweth that he hath but a short time. (Rev. 12:12)

During the Middle Ages (A.D. 476 to 1453), the practice of demonology (or conjuration) was prevalent throughout Europe. According to historical records, many ancient families who regularly practiced magic performed certain incantations which resulted in the appearance of various demons. These demons, who had distinct names, manifested themselves into many different physical forms. It is interesting to note that many of these physical characteristics bear a striking resemblance to our modern day, glowing-eyed monsters and UFO entities. The following list enumerates some of these demonic appearances:

1. *Angels*
2. A raven's head attached to a wolf's body
3. An old man
4. A human figure with wings
5. A lion or a cat
6. A leopard with wings
7. A dog with wings
8. A bull with wings
9. A knight bearing some type of insignia or emblem
10. A duchess
11. A boy
12. A soldier
13. A soldier with a lion's face and glowing eyes

14. A man's face attached to a dog's body with wings
15. A man's face attached to a bull's body with wings
16. A crow with human flesh
17. A dragon with three heads (one being human)
18. A she-wolf with wings

This list also serves to verify the fact that these demons did appear on earth as human beings (male or female), animals (i.e., birds, dogs, cats, wolves, etc.), spiritual beings (angels), hideous creatures with claws and fangs (including a combination of human and animal parts), and numerous other shapes and imitations. Therefore, is it not plausible that the "chupacabras," "Mothman," the "Flatwoods monster," "Momo," and other bizarre creatures that have made thousands of people's hair stand on end could be manifestations of certain demonic spirits? Why are hundreds of residents of Mexico and Puerto Rico afraid to leave their homes at night? Do they suspect that "alien beings" aboard UFOs are mutilating their livestock (for some unknown reason) and that they might be next? Are they afraid of being attacked by some blood-sucking demonic creature?

A sixteenth-century Protestant demonologist, Johan Weyer (1515-1588), estimated that an army of 7,405,926 demons existed and were organized into 1,111 divisions of 6,666 each. It is also interesting that during the Reformation period and the sixteenth-century as well, certain Lutheran leaders calculated a higher number of demons, totaling 2,665,866,746,664 (Melton 1996b). Since their banishment from heaven, are millions of demons lurking in the darkness seeking whom they may devour?

Demonic Possession

Earlier, in chapter three, it was brought to the reader's attention that certain occult practices, such as dabbling with a ouija board, automatic writing, and channeling, may result in the participants becoming possessed by evil entities, commonly known as demons. According to Dr. Malachi Martin (b. 1921), not only can there be "possession" of an individual by a demon, but there also can be oppression by a demon. Father Martin, a best-selling author, is an ex-Jesuit who has performed thousands of exorcisms as a Catholic priest for over thirty years throughout the world.

An exorcism is a ceremony designed to expel a demon from a possessed person by the authority of Jesus Christ. It involves a confrontation between the exorcist—usually, but not limited to, a Catholic priest—and the demon or demons who actually occupy and rule the behavior of an individual or individuals.

People who become "possessed" by a demon have gradually succumbed to that demon's power and evil influence, and, in so doing, their entire being and will are "taken over" by that demon. Fortunately, one cannot be possessed against one's will, and, in reality, most demonic possessions occur through generational transfers. Members of the same family are inhabited by the same demon for generations. Parents actually consign the child to their demon. Subsequently, the child participates in various Satanic ceremonies. Oppression, on the other hand, is when an individual is harassed or bothered continually by a demon (Martin, Dr. Malachi 1996).

It should be pointed out at this juncture that during an exorcism, a nauseating, putrid *odor* may be present in the room where the exorcism is taking place. As previously discussed, an unpleasant odor accompanies various paranormal manifestations, including the evocation of spiritual entities and unearthly hideous creatures associated with UFOs. Is this recurring presence of a putrid odor during paranormal manifestations, in fact, a red flag indicating demonic activity?

Also, during an exorcism, the temperature of the room may fluctuate from extreme heat to extreme cold or vice versa. Since the 1970s, residents of Brazil have witnessed numerous close encounters with UFOs. During these close encounters, a bright, blinding beam of light emanates from the UFO and engulfs an individual. Coincidentally, as this is taking place, the witness is levitated (or pulled up) underneath the unidentified object and in almost all of these instances, *feels the sensation of extreme heat or extreme cold simultaneously* (Pratt 1996). Is this dual hot/cold sensation that takes place during a UFO encounter another red flag signifying that we are, in fact, dealing with demonic forces? It is no wonder that these activities occur since sorcery and spiritualism play a major role in the religious beliefs of thousands of Brazilians. Are demons, in fact, exercising their supernatural powers to materialize "extraterrestrial" spaceships?

As we zoom toward the twenty-first century, demonic activity is becoming more and more prevalent. The supernatural world is intruding on the natural world (cf., Matt. 24). Dr. Malachi Martin reveals an interesting statistic. Since 1975 in the northeastern United States alone, there has been an eight hundred percent increase in demonic possession and oppression. Could this overwhelming increase in the number of people being possessed or oppressed by demons be occurring globally as well? Is this the ultimate Satanic strategy setting up his kingdom with thousands of demonically possessed earthly ambassadors?

Demons apparently choose to appear as hideous creatures with claws and fangs who roam the countryside and attack hundreds of farm animals extracting their blood. The smelly, vampire-like chupacabras of Puerto Rico, Mexico, and Brazil are, in all likelihood, transmogrified fallen angels (i.e., demons).

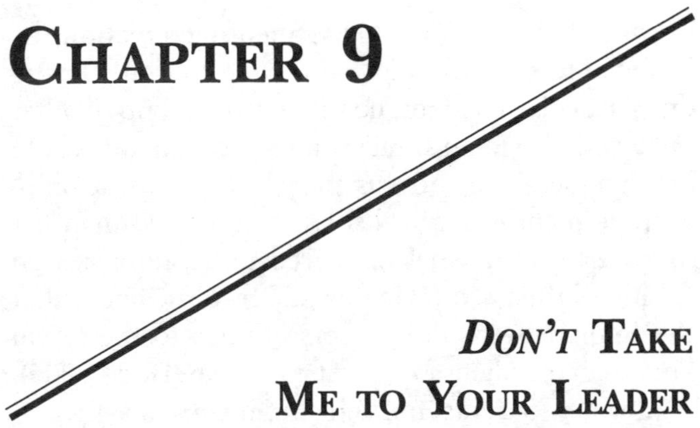

Chapter 9

Don't Take Me to Your Leader

Kidnapped

A series of ongoing paranormal events began unfolding in 1993 for a family of four in Kent, England. The family's eight year old son, "Jason," suddenly and mysteriously became very discontented. He began undergoing a dramatic personality change, exhibiting extreme behavioral disorders both at home and in school. Oddly enough, he was deathly afraid to sleep alone at night. He told his parents that strange men would come into his bedroom and take him away.

According to Jason's testimony, a group of "little men," approximately three-and-a-half feet tall with big heads, big black eyes, long fingers, and bubbly skin, floated through his bedroom window at night and took him to some strange "hospital." One of these men was *taller* than the others.

These mysterious beings then transported him to a cold room, placed him on a table, and stuck needles in him. While undergoing an agonizing medical examination, Jason explained that he felt paralyzed and unable to move. Even though he could not free himself from this tormenting situation, he was able to see what was happening to him. During one particular incident, he witnessed a group of other *children* undergoing similar painful examinations. On another occasion, he was purposely shown a holographic picture which displayed several human beings performing what appeared to be autopsies on several of their kind. He was told by these aliens that the humans were doing worse things to their own kind than the aliens were doing to them (Dodd 1996).

Jason's parents noticed anomalous marks and scars on his body. In addition, he frequently experiences severe nosebleeds. On one occasion, Jason woke up in the middle of the night and began reciting various complex patterns of *numbers,* as if his mind had been pre-programmed. On three other occasions, at precisely 3:30 A.M., the family's dogs began barking and howling as if they were disturbed by something out of the ordinary. Jason's parents awoke each time only to find Jason missing from his bedroom. Twice they found him outside, asleep in the garden. The other time he was asleep in the kitchen.

As if these experiences were not enough, the family reported strange white lights following them as they drive toward their farm. Jason expressed fears that these lights are the "little people" that come and take him away. On several occasions, he witnessed mysterious balls of blue light in his bedroom. Strange noises, similar to poltergeist activity, have been heard throughout the farmhouse by all family members (Dodd 1996). Is Jason, in fact, being abducted by so-called extraterrestrial beings?

Then in 1995, on two separate occasions, an unusual *odor* was present on the family's farm, and several of their cows and horses demonstrated abnormal behavior. When the animals were given food, they refused to eat. Coincidentally, two strange looking individuals dressed in *black* and wearing hats were observed in a field across from the property. Shortly thereafter, several of the cows and horses mysteriously died.

Similar to the experiences of "Jason," in 1970 in Ashburnham, Massachusetts, Betty Andreasson Luca and members of her family frequently witnessed mysterious balls of light floating around inside their house. They also heard strange loud noises. Then on 8 June 1978, two strange looking men were seen standing in their driveway. One of the men was much *taller* than the other and dressed entirely in *black.*

As we have seen, "alien" abductions of humans have been taking place for the past twenty years at an alarming rate throughout the world. What is the reason for the dramatic increase of abductions at this time in history? What is not often disclosed is the fact that *children* are frequently the target of these mysterious abductions.

There's No Generation Gap Here

It is of utmost importance to note at this juncture that many so-called alien abductions are, in fact, generational. The pattern that so often emerges is that a parent is abducted and subsequently his or her child is abducted. As previously mentioned in chapter eight, most *demonic possessions* occur through generational transfers. Are these numerous occurrences of generational abductions another red flag signaling demonic activity? Could *demons,* in fact, be posing as extraterrestrials and abducting entire human families? Are not even *children* exempt from the targeting scanners of these cruel and devilish forces?

In 1989 during an out-of-body experience, Betty Andreasson Luca was escorted to a spaceship by a gray "alien." To her surprise, upon entering a particular room inside this spaceship, she saw her daughter Becky. To Betty's amazement, Becky was sitting in front of some type of viewing screen tracing numerous peculiar symbols that were revealed to her. Betty tried to get her daughter's attention, but was informed by this supposed alien being that Becky could not acknowledge her presence because she was in spirit and Becky was flesh. This "alien" also informed Betty that her daughter was in some type of special training (Fowler 1995). But, training for what? Is Becky's mind being reprogrammed like Jason's? Are these aliens attempting to manipulate and control the wills of *children* for future agendas? Could there be a connection between the mysterious symbols that Becky was tracing and the mysterious numbers Jason recited? Is there a tie-in here with the occult, where numbers and symbols play a unique role?

It should be pointed out that Becky has been the recipient of *automatic writing* since childhood. For years, while in a trancelike state, she has written numerous messages composed of indecipherable pictorial symbols. These pictorial symbols bear a striking resemblance to ancient Egyptian hieroglyphics.

Summer School?

Bestselling author and abductee Whitley Strieber (born 13 June 1945 in San Antonio, Texas) claims that at the age of nine, he was obsessed with books about ancient Egypt. He has also disclosed that during the summer months of his childhood (ages six through twelve), he was mysteriously inducted into a "secret school." He claims that other children participated in these secret school sessions. (In 1995, Strieber discovered that this secret school was, in fact, a real place that once existed in the woods in the Olmos Basin near his childhood home in San Antonio, Texas.)

According to Strieber, the secret school instructors were mysterious old women. They had weird, thin hands and called themselves the "Sisters of Mercy." In 1954 helmets resembling today's Virtual Reality headgear were placed on the children's heads. Strieber supposedly viewed fantastic astronomical events, which he now believes are responsible for the creation of the earth and its subsequent evolution. On another occasion, he found himself in a dark, mysterious jungle inhabited by numerous giant insects. He was gripped with terror when these huge insects began crawling on him (Strieber 1997). Was Whitley Strieber (and many other *children* as well) subjected to alien mind manipulation as far back as the early 1950s?

On 25 January 1967 during Betty Andreasson Luca's initial abduction experience, she observed numerous weird, insect-like creatures crawling up and down buildings located in some otherworldly alien environment.

Mutual Interests

There are many similarities in the abduction accounts of Betty Andreasson Luca and Whitley Strieber. Evidently, they both have been singled out by the UFO phenomenon since childhood. It is not surprising, then, that each have similar interpretations regarding who their abductors are, and why they are here. Essentially, they both feel that their abductors are, in fact, benevolent beings who are visiting the earth for the sole purpose of spiritually guiding humanity into the twenty-first century. In reality, however, might not these entities be more interested in the abductees' *children?* Whitley Strieber does, after all, have a son.

In recent years, numerous books have invaded the market in an attempt to explain the ever-increasing alien abduction phenomenon. Many of these books are written by the abductees themselves (i.e., the experiences of Whitley Strieber). Other books have been written by therapists (i.e., the abduction experiences of Betty Andreasson Luca). In many cases, hypnotic regression techniques have been employed to fully extract the hidden memories of an abductee's experiences. For some unknown reason, an abductee's memory of his or her abduction has been suppressed by these "aliens." Does this infer that the "aliens" are capable of blocking our minds? Is this mental barrier, then, an intentional smoke screen? Do the "aliens," in fact, have a secret hidden agenda that ultimately involves our *children?*

The late Dr. Karla Turner wrote three books describing her and her family's abduction experiences along with those of some immediate friends. Similar to the accounts of Betty Andreasson Luca, Whitley Strieber and many others, Turner uncovered unusual events that took place in her childhood (and the childhood of others) that were associated with the UFO phenomenon.

During her abduction encounters with unusual entities in the 1980s, however, Turner felt that her mind was being "programmed" for a particular mission. Family members and friends had similar feelings. (It is important to note that Turner believed that these unusual creatures were *not* of extraterrestrial, but rather earthly origin.)

On 4 August 1989 this "programming" was realized when she awoke with an overwhelming urge to get out of the city. Two years later, she and her family moved into a house they had built in a sparsely populated area in the backwoods of Arkansas. Interestingly enough, after moving to this wooded area, Turner met thirty other abductees in Arkansas who felt "programmed" to do the same thing.

Mind manipulation appears to be an integral part of the "alien" abduction strategy. Karla Turner, along with friends and members of her family, have described vivid dreams involving the mass arrival of UFOs. Are otherworldly beings, in fact, programming the minds of abductees with visions of carefully concocted future events? Are they readying part of the population for their significant arrival?

Crossbreeding

A mass-programming schedule is also taking place involving the interbreeding of human beings with so-called extraterrestrials. During an abduction experience, the "aliens" often extract sperm and eggs from abductees. They supposedly implant genetically altered fertilized eggs into the womb of female abductees. These female abductees are then abducted one to three months later, and a hybrid fetus is removed from them. Female abductees are often placed in "nursery" rooms occupied by supposed alien-human offspring (which they think are their own). They are instructed to interact with sickly-looking hybrid babies who have weird eyes and oversized heads. Dr. Karla Turner firmly believed that this hybrid scenario was, after all, just a big scam—a type of psychological warfare making these women think that they share offspring with supposed extraterrestrials.

Interestingly enough, Karla's husband claims to have had sexual intercourse with a supposed female alien, who had strikingly human-alien features. In a similar case, a close friend of their son often spoke about an unusual looking woman who would come into his bedroom at night and want to have sex with him.

Sex and the Single Alien

Back in 1957, a Brazilian farmer named Antonio Villas-Boas (now deceased) had a most remarkable abduction experience. He was forcibly taken on board a landed spacecraft by supposed alien beings who had helmets on their heads. He was then stripped of his clothing, and a thick liquid was applied all over his body. After the "aliens" extracted *blood* from his chin, he was left alone in a room with a bed in it. Soon afterwards a beautiful, naked woman (somewhat human in appearance and resembling an Arabian princess) entered the room. According to Villas-Boas, they had sexual relations twice. During the encounter, however, the woman made weird noises similar to "growls" which gave Villas-Boas the impression he was having sex with an animal. Afterwards, the woman pointed to her belly and then to the sky. Did this mean Villas-Boas impregnated a female extraterrestrial? Is it possible she later gave birth to an alien-human offspring? Curiously enough, during the 1970s and the 1980s, many other related abduction cases were reported from Brazil.

On numerous occasions between 1954 and 1963, the late contactee Elizabeth Klarer (1910-1994) allegedly encountered an alien spacecraft with two occupants on board. During one particular incident, she was invited inside this spaceship by "Akon," who she claimed was an extremely handsome extraterrestrial. She embarked on a journey with him to his home planet Meton (located in the solar system of Alpha Centauri). She had sexual relations with Akon and lived on Meton for four months. She claims to have given birth to a male human-alien child, who they named Ayling. She returned to earth and was visited periodically by Akon and Ayling.

Elizabeth Klarer was no ordinary woman. She won numerous awards in art, music, horseback riding, meteorology, and aviation. For five years (1940-1945), she was a pilot in the South African Air Force and was assigned to Royal Air Force Intelligence. Beginning in 1946, she was responsible for the reporting of all UFO sightings to the South African Air Force. Is it just a coincidence that eight years later she would personally be involved in an extraordinary sequence of UFO events? It is interesting to note that, at some point, Klarer believed she was an "extraterrestrial." Did this thought process occur before or after her incredible encounters with UFO entities?

Demon Lovers

Throughout history, there have been numerous accounts of human beings involved in sexual activity with the *Devil* or with *demons.* During the Middle Ages, it was believed that *Satan* empowered his demons to have sexual relations with humans. Even though demons were generally considered to be sexless, there was widespread belief that they could assume human form (either male or female).

In the study of demonology, a demon that takes the form of a woman and has sexual relations with a human male is called a *succubus.* A demon that takes the form of a man and has sexual relations with human females is called an *incubus.*

In most incubi or succubi encounters, the human form envisioned is of great beauty and countenance. History has bequeathed us with numerous accounts of demons appearing as beautiful young girls to their male human lovers and handsome men to their female human lovers. Witnesses also reported that these demonic "look-a-likes" often changed into hideous monsters (like the UFO entities of the twentieth century). It is also interesting to note that historical records dating back hundreds of years contain numerous accounts involving incubi/succubi interbreeding with human beings.

Even today, there are astounding accounts of human beings having sexual relations with supposed alien beings. During these "alien" abduction experiences, the interbreeding of humans with these so-called extraterrestrials often takes place (or, at least, the abductee is made to think that this is happening). Are these incredible encounters just another facet of the overall demonic program, incorporating the incubus/succubus motif? Have they latched onto a development of the human imagination, or have they, in fact, inspired it all along? Is this yet another circle in the web of demonic deception—abducting millions throughout the world?

Abducted

The bizarre encounters during an abduction experience are often devastating to an individual. Abductees often become emotionally distraught and feel victimized. They live in constant fear that they will be abducted again and again. As previously noted, many abductees are subjected to bizarre medical examinations during which devices are often used to extract sperm and ova. After these unpleasant examinations are over, abductees often feel sexually violated.

It is interesting to note that in the majority of abduction cases, the abductors (usually more than one) are described as small gray beings with oversized heads and big slanted eyes. During the beginning of an abduction experience, abductees often witness a glowing light coming through their bedroom window. These mysterious beings usually appear inside this source of light. Many abductees, however, first report seeing these creatures as animals (i.e., wolves, monkeys, owls, or other animals). Others have reported seeing "angels" or "devils." These figures suddenly appear as small, gray humanoid beings. After making eye contact, one of these beings touches the witness, and he or she is engulfed by this peculiar light and begins to float into it. The abductee is then escorted out through the bedroom window (either open or closed) or through a wall or ceiling. Subsequently, he or she is taken to the source of the light which, in almost all cases, is a circular UFO.

Once aboard this UFO, the witness is placed on a table inside a circular examining room (which closely resembles the operating room of a hospital). They then undergo a rigorous medical examination which lasts approximately twenty minutes. Witnesses often report seeing hundreds of other human beings undergoing similar examinations.

It appears that the sole mission of these "alien" beings is to efficiently perform medical procedures on numerous helpless human subjects. Evidently, part of the "alien" agenda is experimenting with our physical bodies. Perhaps this obsession with our *physical* bodies is just a smoke screen covering their real intention, which is to get to our psyche! In numerous abduction cases, witnesses are angry and terrified. They feel they have been subjected to both physical and psychological torture. Interestingly enough, overseeing these medical experiments is a *taller* being who appears to be supervising the whole operation. Is this being *Satan* himself? Are the smaller beings, then, his minions, the *demons?*

CHAPTER 10

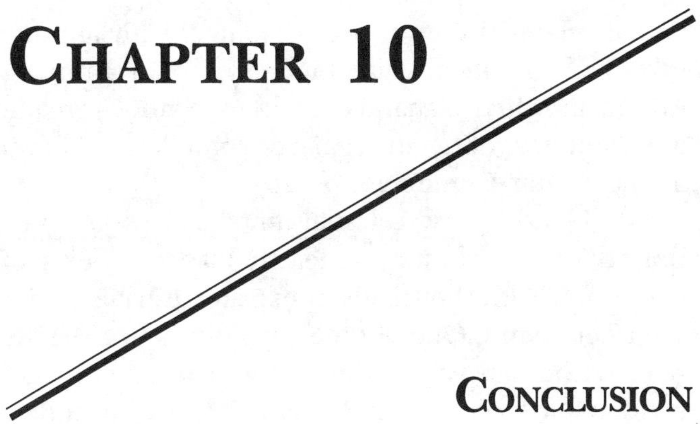

CONCLUSION

The Secret Mission

The preceding nine chapters have intricately pieced together the monumental evidence regarding the UFO phenomenon. The facts that have been uncovered clearly reveal just how the UFO phenomenon is inextricably linked with the occult, demonology, and the New Age movement. Indeed, something unimaginable is going on that affects you and me. An elaborate *sinister* scheme, which germinated in the late 1940s, is now blossoming as this century nears its end.

As a result of this devious masterminded plot, millions of people around the globe are anxiously awaiting the first public landings of so-called extraterrestrial spaceships. They honestly believe that on board are benevolent extraterrestrial beings who are significantly more advanced than us humans. These extraterrestrial "saviors" are going to guide us into the twenty-first century. Thousands of New Age disciples are, in fact, communicating with these "extraterrestrials" via channeling, automatic writing, trance mediumship, and other *occult* means. These individuals claim that they are in contact with an elite group of extraterrestrials, namely, Sanat Kumara, Maitreya, Ashtar, Sananda, Kuthumi, Saint Germain, and even *Jesus* of the intergalactic confederacy known as the Ashtar Command.

Right now these celestial ambassadors are purported to be orbiting the earth in great fleets of spaceships with thousands of extraterrestrials under their command. One of their missions is to evacuate selected human *souls* during cataclysmic events that are soon to occur on earth. How are we to understand these events? Are these beings, in fact, really extraterrestrials? Will they arrive just in time to save us from our own destruction? Will we soon witness mass landings of UFOs?

Meanwhile, in various parts of the world, mysterious human-animal mutilations linked to smelly vampire-like creatures are being reported in the same geographical locations in which UFOs are being reported. Even more horrific, thousands of families are being abducted repeatedly by small, grey "alien" beings with oversized heads and weird eyes. These abductees are being subjected to painful physical examinations along with various types of mind manipulation. Apparently, these "extraterrestrials" are playing the role of Dr. Jekyll and Mr. Hyde. Are these creatures from the netherworld transforming themselves and deceiving us into thinking that they are an advanced race of extraterrestrials?

The supernatural world has strategically invaded our physical world. Our curiosity with the occult has turned into dabbling, which has opened the door into the unknown. Mysterious supernatural entities are thereby being welcomed into our reality with open arms. Unfortunately, like the vampires of old, once these "creatures" are given sway, they then begin to exert unlimited physical and psychic power over an individual or group.

The dreaded Apocalypse, as foretold in the Bible's prophetic book of Revelation, is likely just around the corner. Increased *demonic* activity is part and parcel of the end times scenario. Who knows what the creative, sinister genius of *Satan* and his hordes will devise to allure and deceive us? These beings are on the march, seeking to devour us, knowing their time is running out. The twentieth century mind has been carefully and cunningly manipulated and has now been successfully convinced that an advanced race of extraterrestrials is at work.

These UFO entities that have been contacting and abducting certain human individuals during this century are, however, not extraterrestrial beings from another planet. Those mysterious cavorting lights parading in our night skies are, therefore, not extraterrestrial spacecraft at all. It is just a show, like a firework display. And, it is a very clever design indeed. The "secret mission" of the UFOs is to ultimately deceive the entire population into thinking that we are being visited by benevolent extraterrestrials. Sadly, they even want us to believe that the historical Jesus Christ is an extraterrestrial.

Through Heaven's Gate?

The terrible mass suicide that made headlines in March 1997 brought the Heaven's Gate cult into the public eye, but they have a long history. Over twenty years ago, back in 1975, Marshall Herff Applewhite, the cult leader and mystic guru, along with his counterpart Bonnie Lu Trusdale Nettles, emerged on the UFO scene by forming a "religious" UFO cult called Human Individual Metamorphosis (HIM).

Here again, religious overtones abound. HIM's goal was to teach members how to reach the "next level" (i.e., the "Evolutionary Level Above Human") where they could obtain *eternal life.* To achieve this goal, anyone who joined HIM was subjected to "the Process," whereby an individual was required to renounce all earthly possessions. Communication with extraterrestrial beings who existed in this "higher level" (i.e., heaven) soon followed. After contact was made, various members of HIM were instructed by these outer space entities to carry out a specific "mission."

Curiously, during the 1970s, Applewhite and Nettles both claimed they underwent a physical and spiritual *transformation.* As a result, they truly believed that they were the two witnesses recorded in the biblical book of Revelation (cf., Rev. 11: 3-6). Subsequently, they changed their names to "Bo" (Applewhite) and "Peep" (Nettles) and were referred to by their followers as "the Two." In a similar vein, many of their followers adopted biblical names including John the Beloved, Peter, David, Joshua, Judas the Lesser, and Jason.

Bo and Peep recounted to their followers that they were indeed heavenly messengers sent to earth by the "Father." They proceeded to embark on a "spiritual mission" similar to the account of the two witnesses spoken of in Revelation (cf., Rev. 11). As in the account in Revelation 11, they believed that at some point in time during their earthly mission, a "demonstration" would occur in which they would be assassinated. After three and a half days, they would rise from the dead (vv. 7-12), enter a UFO, and ascend into heaven, paralleling the resurrection of Jesus Christ that occurred two thousand years ago. However, this spectacular "demonstration" never occurred.

It is not surprising that Applewhite and Nettles attempted to connect key biblical revelations to the UFO phenomenon. Throughout their lives, they were heavily influenced by such *occult* practices as astrology, healing, meditation, metaphysics, Eastern mysticism, and theosophy. Nettles even claimed that she was in direct contact with a deceased monk named Brother Francis who continually guided her as she interpreted various astrological charts.

In the mid-1980s, Bo and Peep changed their names to "Do" and "Ti" and renamed their group the "Total Overcomers." Ti (Nettles) died in the 1980s, and the group later became known as Heaven's Gate. Three-and-a-half days before *Easter* (26 March 1997), members of the Heaven's Gate cult committed mass suicide in a noble attempt to leave the earth and rendezvous with an extraterrestrial spaceship trailing Comet Hale-Bopp. Events like this jar us into realizing the *sinister* nature of this phenomenon.

The Secret Mission Continues

It is particularly intriguing that UFO-related events are continually saturated with religious symbolism. If the nature of these beings was genuinely extraterrestrial in origin, they would certainly relate to the human race on a scientific level, owing to our advances and confidence in science. Covert activity, such as has been witnessed for more than fifty years, seems out of character. Certainly the scientific community would be the most likely segment to accept and affirm their identity, wouldn't they? What if this extraterrestrial "appearance" is no more than a costume? What if, in fact, they are just waiting for the right moment in time? What if their timetable coincides with the emergence of the "anti-Christ?"

The conditioning process has yielded its fruit in due season. It has resulted in the belief that advanced extraterrestrials, *our friends and helpers,* are visiting our planet. But, what have they actually done to help us? Their "save the planet" activities have, in reality, just allowed time to be on their side. Their "commander in chief" might just be waiting to give them their final mission briefing. A "mass appearance" of extraterrestrial spaceships may, in fact, signify the beginning of the Apocalypse. In the meantime, their "secret mission" is advancing right on schedule, convincing as many people as possible that they are indeed extraterrestrials.

The New World Order

We are now witnessing the rapid formation of a one-world economy, the cornerstone of an emerging "New World Order." Organizations such as the Aetherius Society, the Tara Center, Share International Foundation, Lucis Trust and many others who have been influenced by theosophical teachings and "extraterrestrial" contact are promoting and supporting the establishment of this "New World Order." Lord Maitreya is being promoted as "the Christ" and currently channels messages through Tuella and others involved with the Ashtar Command. His channeled messages reveal a "Divine Plan" which initiated the development of this "New World Order," according to which Lord Maitreya is apparently planning to set up his kingdom on earth. Perhaps he will be the ruler of this "New World Order." What if Lord Maitreya is, in fact, the anti-Christ incarnate?

As we approach the twenty-first century, the glorious "New Age" that millions of people have eagerly anticipated is coming upon us. The "New World Order" is rapidly becoming a reality. This may just be the key ingredient that ultimately sets the stage for the appearance of the anti-Christ and heralded by a fleet of spaceships.

Signs of the End of the Age

In the New Testament of the Bible, Jesus reveals through Matthew (cf., Matt. 24), Mark (cf., Mark 13), and Luke (cf., Luke 21) the various signs that will lead to the end of this age. Even though only God the Father knows when that time will be (cf., Matt. 24:36), Jesus gives us ample warnings, followed by general signs that signify the end is about to occur.

We appear to be teetering on the edge of the precipice. Just turn on CNN and watch the multitude of sins of a civilization whose heart has grown cold (cf., Matt. 24:12). Despite our technological advancements, thousands continue to die from famine, war, and disease (cf., Matt. 24:6-7). Pay your local New Age bookstore a visit, and you will discover thousands of channeled manuscripts claiming that certain supposed extraterrestrial beings (i.e., Sananda, Maitreya, ESU, and Sanat Kumara) are Jesus the Christ (cf., Matt. 24:5, 23-24). You will find books on the black arts (i.e., witchcraft, sorcery, magic, Satanism, necromancy, etc.) which teach you how to conjure up supernatural entities (cf., Deut. 18:9-14).

Even societies that were once anchored in a God-fearing and biblically-based value system are careening down the road to destruction after the likes of Sodom and Gomorrah (cf., Gen. 13-19). By dabbling in the occult, millions of people may just be evoking supernatural entities and directing them into our reality. What if these supernatural entities are, in fact, *demonic* beings? What if these old familiar friends are just familiar spirits? What if they are actually attempting to carry out a global, master-minded mission?

Sananda's outerspace confederacy known as the Ashtar Command boasts great fleets of spaceships occupying thousands of well-organized ranks of extraterrestrials. These so-called extraterrestrials are channeling messages to thousands of New Age disciples who, in turn, are spreading a bogus intergalactic gospel of salvation to humanity.

It is not surprising, then, that these twentieth century legions of extraterrestrials bear a striking resemblance to the various ranks of *demons* that were organized into specific groups by demonologists during the Middle Ages. These demonologists surmised that *Satan* was "commander in chief" of an army of demons consisting of 2,400 legions. Certain demons of rank also commanded numerous legions.

The Bible also speaks of well-organized ranks of demons (cf., Eph. 6:11-12) who ultimately disseminate false doctrines during the end times (cf., I Tim. 4:1-3). Is it just a coincidence that Ashtar, Soltec, Monka, Korton, and Athena have distinct rankings as associates of the Ashtar Command? Are they not, in fact, channeling distorted doctrines to the New Age community?

A False Message to Humanity: The Satanic Rapture?

For the past two decades, direct communications with various members of the Ashtar Command by numerous New Age leaders has resulted in a special mission to be carried out by New Age followers.

These New Age disciples (also known as the "Forces of Light," the "Souls of Light," the "Light Workers," and members of the "Intergalactic Legion of Special Volunteers") are undertaking a "spiritual" assignment on earth (i.e., Lord Maitreya's "Divine Plan"). The purpose of this "on earth assignment" is to spread (possibly via the Internet) the intergalactic gospel of salvation to millions of people around the globe. Supposedly, our planet will soon undergo a spiritual and physical transformation. The earth will be "cleansed" and a "higher level of consciousness" will be attained by those who are enlightened by this New Age philosophy.

Upon completion of the cleansing of the planet, Armageddon will occur and the Ashtar Command's fleet of spaceships will herald in "Christ's" return. A "global evacuation" will subsequently take place, and all *souls* who qualify (i.e., by walking in the "Light") will be lifted off the planet's surface and transported aboard Ashtar's fleet of spaceships. Total evacuation is estimated to occur in about fifteen minutes.

Interestingly enough, there are three phases in the schedule involving the "global evacuation of souls." Phase I is the first evacuation. All spiritual leaders and teachers of the New Age movement will be the first ones beamed up to the spaceships. Phase II, occurring shortly after Phase I, signals the evacuation of *children* along with those who have followed and heeded New Age doctrine. Phase III heralds humanity's final rescue. Thousands of spaceships will hover low enough in the skies for all to see. Some of these ships will then land, and everyone who is not afraid will be invited on board . . .

Will you be among them?

APPENDIX

by Pastor Tom Vasiliow

> We know that God causes everything to work together for the good of those who love God and are called according to his purpose for them, and I am convinced that nothing can ever separate us from his love. Death cannot, and life cannot. The angels can't, and the demons can't. Our fears for today, our worries about tomorrow, and even the powers of hell can't keep God's love away. Whether we are high above the sky or in the deepest ocean, nothing in all creation will ever be able to separate us from the love of God that is revealed in Christ Jesus our Lord (Rom. 8:28, 38-39 NLT).

"Angels of light" abound in our time in history. While the spirit of the Antichrist has been with us since New Testament times, and many antichrists have arisen since then (cf., I John 2:18-22; 4:1-3), the activity of Satan and his demons can be expected to increase as we near the end of time as we know it (cf., Matt. 24). Not only has their activity increased, but their strategy and *modus operandi* has increased as well (cf., II Cor. 2:11). The supernatural is intruding upon the natural world at an alarming rate.

We should neither be surprised nor alarmed because "the god of this world has blinded the minds of the unbelieving, that they might not see the light of the gospel of the glory of Christ, who is the image of

God" (II Cor. 4:4 NAS). The whole world is under the control of the evil one (cf., I John 5:19b NIV), and it is not surprising that as Satan's time is running out, his efforts are being multiplied and expanded.

Over twenty-five years of intense investigation into this phenomenon has, at times, spawned more questions than answers, but we should not be afraid to ask the hard questions and evaluate their answers in light of the revelation given to us by God in His word, the Bible. The Bible clearly portrays an adversary stalking around, seeking people to devour (cf., I Pet. 4:8). But it also declares that we can resist him, by staying firm in our faith (cf., I Pet. 4:9), and he will flee from us (cf., James 4:7). His activity is widespread, from the garden (cf., Gen. 3) to the grand finale (cf., Rev. 20). He wreaks havoc on humanity (cf., Eph. 2:2; 6:12ff), yet we can bear our armor from God to fight him (cf., Eph. 6:11) and raise our shield to defend ourselves from his arrows (cf., Eph. 6:16).

For some mysterious reason known only to God, Satan has been allowed to roam freely on the earth (cf., Job 1:7; 2:2) as part of a grander plan. Our ultimate comfort and consolation lie in the assurance that his doom is sealed (cf., Matt. 25:41; Rev. 20:10) and that our eternal destiny is in the presence of the Lord (cf., Matt. 25:21, 46; John 3:16), where we will have His joy (cf., Ps. 16:11) and enjoy Him forever!

After reading this book, it would be easy to conclude that Satan, along with his minions, the demons, are, perhaps, the most powerful forces in the supernatural realm. However, the good news is that Jesus, the Son of God, is the King of Kings and Lord of Lords and ruler even over Satan himself!

We learn from the book of Job that Satan's power is limited, controlled, and operates only by the permission of God (Job 1:7-12; 2:1-7). Satan and his evil hosts were defeated finally and ultimately when Jesus was crucified on the cross. He shed His blood so that we could be forgiven of our sins and brought into a personal relationship with God. Jesus in Matthew 10:28 tells us "And do not be afraid of those who want to kill you. They can only kill your body; they cannot touch your soul. Fear only God, who can destroy both soul and body in hell" (NLT). These words are often viewed as words of condemnation when, in fact, they contain words of assurance as well. If we place our "soul" in the care of God who loves us, no being alive, human or demonic, can ultimately destroy us.

According to the Bible, we mortals are going to put on immortality, the perishable putting on the imperishable (1 Cor. 15:33). As a result of disobedience and sin, death has stung the whole human race, but the good news is that even death may be swallowed up in victory. We can give thanks to God who gives us this victory through the Lord Jesus Christ (1 Cor. 15:55-57).

The gospel (good news) was announced so that "you may believe that Jesus is the Christ, the Son of God; and that believing you may have life in His name." (John 20:31 NAS). We are also reminded that "God showed His great love for us by sending Christ to die for us while we were still sinners. And since we have been made right in God's sight by the blood of Christ, he will certainly save us from God's judgement. For since we were restored to friendship with God by the death of His Son while we were still his enemies, we will certainly be delivered from eternal punishment by his life" (Rom. 5:8-10 NLT).

If this book has provided some food for thought, and even inspired you to consider or reconsider the real Jesus Christ, I would encourage you to call on His name. Then you need not be concerned about being invited on board a spacecraft. You will receive the greatest invitation known to humankind: ". . . if anyone hears my voice and opens the door, I will come in . . ." (Rev. 3:20). These are the people who have entered into a relationship with the true and living God.

And you will be among them.

Bibliography of Sources

Adamski, George. *Inside the Space Ships.* Great Britain: Neville Spearman, 1966.

American Heritage Dictionary, The Third Edition. Houghton Mifflin Company, 1992.

Ankerberg, John, and John Weldon. *The Facts On the Occult—Answers To Tough Questions About Spiritism, Occult Phenomena, & Psychic Powers.* Eugene, OR: Harvest House Publishers, 1991.

_____. *The Facts On UFO'S and Other Supernatural Phenomena—Answers To the Most Asked Questions.* Eugene, OR: Harvest House Publishers, 1992.

Art Bell After Dark (Monthly Newsletter). Various Editions. Central Point, OR: Chancellor Broadcasting Company, 1996.

Ashtar Command. *New World Order: Prophecies from Space.* New Brunswick, NJ: Inner Light Publications, 1990.

Barker, Gray. *They Knew Too Much About Flying Saucers.* New York: University Books, 1956.

Begich, Nick. "The Very Real Dangers of HAARP." *Art Bell After Dark,* vol. 2, no. 4 (April 1996): 6-12.

Begich, Nick, and Jeane Manning. *Angels Don't Play This Haarp: Advances In Tesla Technology.* Anchorage, Alaska: Earthpulse Press, 1995.

Bender, Albert K. *Flying Saucers and the Three Men,* Clarksburg, WV: Saucerian Books, 1962.

Bethurum, Truman. *Aboard a Flying Saucer,* Los Angeles, CA: DeVorss & Co., 1954.

Bishop, Gregory, and Wesley Nations. "Taken—For a Ride: Karla Turner Doctors the Message." *The Excluded Middle* (Issue no. 4, 1995): 8-11, 39-41.

Brooke, Tal. *When the World Will Be As One: The Coming New World Order (*Eugene, OR: Harvest House Publishers, Inc., 1989).

Cheetam, Erika. *The Further Prophecies of Nostradamus: 1985 and Beyond,* New York: The Putnam Publishing Group, 1985.

_____. *The Prophecies of Nostradamus.* New York: G.P. Putnam's Sons, 1973.

Clark, Jerome. *The Emergence of a Phenomenon: UFOs from the Beginning through 1959—The UFO Encyclopedia, volume 2.* Detroit, MI: Omnigraphics, 1992.

_____. *High Strangeness: UFOs from 1960 through 1979—The UFO Encyclopedia, Volume 3.* Detroit, MI: Omnigraphics, 1996.

_____. *UFOs in the 1980s: The UFO Encyclopedia, Volume 1.* Detroit, MI: Apogee Books, 1990.

_____. *Unexplained! 347 Strange Sightings, Incredible Occurrences, and Puzzling Physical Phenomena.* Detroit, MI: Visible Ink Press, 1993.

Clark, Jerome, and Marcello Truzzi. *UFO Encounters: Sightings, Visitations, and Investigations.* Lincolnwood, IL: Publications International, Ltd., 1992.

Collings, Beth, and Anna Jamerson. *Connections: Solving Our Alien Abduction Mystery.* Newberg, OR: Wild Flower Press, 1996.

The Concise Columbia Encyclopedia, The Columbia University Press, 1991.

Corrales, Scott. *The Chupacabras Diaries: An Official Chronicle of Puerto Rico's Paranormal Predator.* Derrick City, PA: Samizdat Press, 1996.

_____. "Showing Its Hand: The U.S. Military and UFOs in Puerto Rico." *The Excluded Middle* (Issue no. 4, 1995): 29-31, 43.

Crockett, Arthur. *Secret Prophecy of Fatima Revealed!* New York: Global Communications, 1982.

Curtiss, Harriette Augusta and F. Homer. *The Key to the Universe.* Albuquerque: Sun Publishing Co., 1917.

Davenport, Marc. *Visitors From Time: The Secret of the UFOs.* Tigard, OR: Wild Flower Press, 1992.

Davidson, Gustav. *A Dictionary of Angels: Including the Fallen Angels.* New York: The Free Press, 1967.

Davis, Vance A., with Brian Blashaw. *Unbroken Promises: A True Story of Courage and Belief.* Mesa, AZ: White Mesa Publishers, 1995.

Derenberger, Woodrow W., and Harold W. Hubbard. *Visitors From Lanulos.* New York: Vantage Press, 1971.

Dodd, Tony. "The Abduction of Jason Williams." *UFO Magazine* [Quest] (March/April 1996): 30, 31, 36, 37, 39.

Dongo, Tom. *The Alien Tide: Mysteries of Sedona, Book II.* Sedona, AZ: Hummingbird Publishing Co., 1990.

Edwards, Frank. *Strange World.* Secaucus, NJ: Citadel Press, 1964.

Emenegger, Robert. *UFOs Past, Present and Future.* New York: Ballantine Books, 1974.

Fowler, Raymond E. *The Watchers: The Secret Design Behind UFO Abduction.* New York: Bantam Books, 1990.

_____. *The Watchers II: Exploring UFOs and the Near-Death Experience.* Newberg, OR: Wild Flower Press, 1995.

Freixedo, Salvador. "Defendamonos De Los Dioses." *Nemesis: The Chupacabras at Large, A Samizdat Update* (Summer 1996): 21-32.

Gaynor, Frank, ed., *Dictionary of Mysticism.* New York: Philosophical Library, 1953.

George, Leonard. *Alternative Realities: The Paranormal, the Mystic and the Transcendent in Human Experience.* New York: Facts On File, Inc., 1995.

Greenfield, Allen H. *Secret Cipher of the UFOnauts.* Lilburn, GA: IllumiNet Press, 1994.

Guiley, Rosemary Ellen. *Harper's Encyclopedia of Mystical & Paranormal Experience.* New York: HarperCollins Publishers, 1991.

Hagee, John. *Day of Deception: Separating Truth from Falsehood in These Last Days.* Nashville, TN: Thomas Nelson Publishers, 1997.

Hall, Richard. *Uninvited Guests: A Documented History of UFO Sightings, Alien Encounters & Coverups.* Santa Fe, NM: Aurora Press, 1988.

_____, ed. *The UFO Evidence.* Washington, DC: National Investigations Committee on Aerial Phenomena, 1964.

Hopkins, Budd. *Intruders: The Incredible Visitations At Copley Woods.* New York: Ballantine Books, 1987.

Howe, Linda Moulton. "Chupacabras: The Mysterious Bloodsuckers." *Art Bell After Dark*, vol. 2, no. 7 (July 1996): 10-13.

Jacobs, David M. *Secret Life: Firsthand Accounts of UFO Abductions.* New York: Simon & Schuster, 1992.

Julien, Nadia. *The Mammoth Dictionary of Symbols.* New York: Carroll & Graf Publishers, Inc., 1989.

Keel, John A. *Disneyland of the Gods.* New York: Amok Press, 1988.

_____. *The Eighth Tower.* New York: Saturday Review Press/E.P. Dutton & Co., 1975a.

_____. *The Mothman Prophecies.* New York: Saturday Review Press/E.P. Dutton & Co., 1975b.

_____. *Our Haunted Planet.* Greenwich, CT: Fawcett Publications, Inc., 1971.

_____. *Strange Creatures from Time and Space.* Great Britain: Neville Spearman, 1975c.

_____. *UFOs: Operation Trojan Horse.* New York: G.P. Putnam's Sons, 1970.

Keith, Jim. *Casebook on Alternative 3: UFOs, Secret Societies and World Control.* Lilburn, GA: IllumiNet Press, 1994.

Keyhoe, Donald E. *Aliens from Space: The Real Story of Unidentified Flying Objects.* Garden City, NY: Doubleday & Company, Inc., 1973.

Keyhoe, Donald E., and Gordon I. R. Lore, Jr., eds. *Strange Effects from UFOs.* Washington, DC: National Investigations Committee on Aerial Phenomena, 1969.

Lady Queenborough (Edith Starr Miller). *Occult Theocracy.* Los Angeles: The Christian Book Club of America, 1933.

Leslie, Desmond, and George Adamski. *Flying Saucers Have Landed.* New York: The British Book Center, 1953.

Lewis, James R., ed. *The Gods Have Landed.* Albany: State University of New York Press, 1995.

Lost Books of the Bible and the Forgotten Books of Eden, The. World Bible Publishers, Inc.

Lindsey, Hal. *Satan is Alive and Well on Planet Earth.* Grand Rapids, MI: The Zondervan Corporation, 1972.

_____. *There's A New World Coming.* Santa Ana: Vision House Publishers, 1973.

Mandelker, Scott. *From Elsewhere: Being E.T. in America.* New York: Birch Lane Press by Carol Publishing Group, 1995.

Marrs, Texe. *Texe Marrs' Book of New Age Cults and Religions.* Austin, TX: Living Truth Publishers, 1990.

Martin, Jorge. "The Chupacabras Phenomenon." *UFO Magazine* [Quest] (March/April 1996): 20-26.

Martin, Malachi. "Coast to Coast AM" w/Art Bell, Program #961018C (cassette series). Central Point, OR: Chancellor Broadcasting Company, 1996.

Mather, George A., Larry A. Nichols, and Alvin J. Schmidt. *Dictionary of Cults, Sects, Religions and the Occult.* Grand Rapids, MI: Zondervan Publishing House, 1993.

McCloy, James F., and Ray Miller, Jr. *The Jersey Devil.* Wilmington, DE: The Middle Atlantic Press, Inc., 1976.

Melton, J. Gordon. *Encyclopedia of American Religions.* Fifth Edition. Detroit: Gale Research, 1996a.

_____, ed. *Encyclopedia of Occultism & Parapsychology.* Fourth Edition. Detroit: Gale Research, 1996b.

_____. *The Vampire Book: The Encyclopedia of the Undead.* Detroit: Visible Ink Press, 1994.

Melton, J. Gordon, Jerome Clark, and Aidan A. Kelly. *New Age Encyclopedia.* Detroit: Gale Research, 1990.

Menger, Howard. *From Outer Space to You.* Clarksburg, WV: Saucerian Books, 1959.

Milanovich, Norma J., with Betty Rice and Cynthia Ploski. *We, The Arcturians.* Albuquerque, NM: Athena Publishing, 1990.

Mysteries of Mind Space & Time: The Unexplained. 26 vols. Westport, CT: H. S. Stuttman Inc., 1992.

O'Brien, Christopher. *The Mysterious Valley.* New York: St. Martin's Press, 1996.

Parker, Derek and Julia. *The Compleat Astrologer.* New York: Bantam Books, Inc., 1971.

Pratt, Bob. *UFO Danger Zone: Terror and Death in Brazil—Where Next?* Madison, WI: Horus House Press, Inc., 1996.

Rand, McNally & Co. *Rand McNally Road Atlas.* Chicago: Rand McNally & Company, 1983.

Randle, Kevin D. *A History of UFO Crashes.* New York: Avon Books, 1995.

Sachs, Margaret. *The UFO Encyclopedia.* New York: G. P. Putnam's Sons, 1980.

Sanderson, Ivan T. *Invisible Residents: A Disquisition Upon Certain Matters Maritime, and the Possibility of Intelligent Life Under the Waters of This Earth.* New York: World Publishing Company, 1970.

Smith, Wes. "At War With the Demon: The Strife of Exorcism." *Art Bell After Dark*, vol. 3, no. 1 (January 1997): 4-6.

Spence, Lewis. *An Encyclopedia of Occultism.* New York: Citadel Press, 1960.

Spencer, John. *The UFO Encyclopedia.* New York: Avon Books, 1991.

Stevens, Wendelle C. "The Greatest UFO Wave in History Over Mexico Now." *International UFO Library*, vol. 3, no. 1 (3rd Anniversary Issue 1994): 8, 9, 51.

Stranges, Frank E. *My Friend from Beyond Earth.* Van Nuys, CA: I.E.C., Inc., 1960.

_____. *The Stranger at the Pentagon.* Van Nuys, CA: I.E.C., Inc., 1967.

Strieber, Whitley. *Communion: A True Story.* New York: Avon Books, 1987.

_____. *The Secret School: Preparation For Contact.* New York: HarperCollins Publishers, Inc., 1997.

_____. *Transformation: The Breakthrough.* New York: Avon Books, 1988.

Stuart, John. *UFO Warning.* Clarksburg, WV: Saucerian Books, 1963.

Supernatural, The. 19 vols. London: Aldus Books Limited, 1976.

Thompson's Chain-Reference Bible. Indianapolis: B.B. Kirkbride Bible Co., Inc., 1964.

Tuella (pseudonym of Thelma B. Terrell), ed. *A New Book of Revelations.* New Brunswick, NJ: Inner Light Publications, 1995.

_____, ed. *Ashtar.* New Brunswick, NJ: Inner Light Publications, 1994.

_____, ed. *Cosmic Prophecies for the Year 2,000.* New Brunswick, NJ: Inner light Publications, 1994.

_____, ed. *On Earth Assignment.* New Brunswick, NJ: Inner Light Publications, 1994.

_____, ed. *Project World Evacuation.* New Brunswick, NJ: Inner Light Publications, 1993.

Turner, Karla. *Into the Fringe: A True Story of Alien Abduction.* New York: The Berkley Publishing Group, 1992.

Turner, Karla, with Ted Rice. *Masquerade of Angels.* Roland, AR: Kelt Works, 1994.

Twitchell, Cleve. *The UFO Saga.* Lakemont, GA: CSA Press, 1966.

Vallee, Jacques. *Dimensions: A Casebook of Alien Contact.* Chicago: Contemporary Books, Inc., 1988.

_____. *Messengers of Deception: UFO Contacts and Cults.* Berkeley: And/Or Press, 1979.

_____. *Passport to Magonia: From Folklore to Flying Saucers.* Chicago: Henry Regnery Company, 1969.

_____. *Revelations: Alien Contact and Human Deception.* New York: Ballantine Books, 1991.

Walters, Ed, and Frances Walters. *UFO Abductions in Gulf Breeze.* New York: Avon Books, 1994.

Weldon, John, and Zola Levitt. *UFOs: What On Earth Is Happening?* Irvine, CA: Harvest House Publishers, 1975.

Williamson, George Hunt. *The Saucers Speak: A Documentary Report of Interstellar Communication by Radiotelegraphy.* Great Britain: Neville Spearman, 1963.

World Book Encyclopedia, The. 20 vols. Chicago: Field Enterprises, Inc., 1966.

INDEX

B

C

N

O

P

Q

R

S

T

U

For Further Information

If you would like to contact the author, please write to the following address:

Paul Christopher
P.O. Box 10788
Glendale, AZ 85318